STRUGGLE

— & —

STRENGTH

*Eight Ordinary Women
with Lives Most Unusual*

*To my southern Arizona
neighbors,
I hope you enjoy these
stories. Sharon K.*

SHARON A. KENNEDY

Struggle and Strength: Eight Ordinary Women with Lives Most Unusual

Published by Wheatmark®
2030 East Speedway Boulevard, Suite 106
Tucson, Arizona 85719 USA
www.wheatmark.com

ISBN: 978-1-62787-665-0
ISBN: 978-1-62787-666-7
LCCN: 2018912946

The true wisdom of life consists in
seeing the extraordinary in the ordinary.

—Pearl Buck

DEDICATION

To my sister, Sandra Kennedy Strain, who has risen from losses
in her life more times than I can count.

CONTENTS

ACKNOWLEDGMENTS

The genesis of this book began four years ago, not long after my retirement. I had written one book simply because I believed that story needed to be told. I realized then how much I enjoyed listening to people and telling their stories. My next opportunity came in my new hometown, Charlotte, Michigan (pop. 9,200), when Travis Silvis, editor of the *County Journal,* a small Eaton County newspaper, allowed me to write a monthly 500-word article. I wrote under the byline Musings from the Newbie on what it was like to be a new resident. I was smitten by that experience. People liked the articles about people and things I found interesting. I wrote a hundred-year perspective under the title of *Women of the Land* by finding stories in the history of the area through interviews with much older women or younger women who told me about their mothers. This process started me on the path to the current book about women. I am grateful to Travis Silvis.

Interviews take time. In addition to the women profiled, I am grateful to the following people who gave willingly of their time: Sherry Forrest, Christopher Harton, Ed Thomas, Jane White, Liz Nobis, Diana Catallo, and Dan Durkee. As a new writer, I have a lot of learning to do on the craft of writing. In this regard, I am grateful to Judy Bridges, author and owner of Red Bird Studios, a writing studio in Milwaukee, Wisconsin. While attending a one-week Writer's Retreat in Ellison Bay, Door County, Wisconsin, in 2016, Judy forced me to write the first four pages of one of the stories and have it critiqued by others at the retreat. I would have been perfectly content to do an outline and research. Her insistence was the impetus I needed to finish writing that story and seven more.

During two summers, I availed myself of the Writers Retreat at Interlochen College of Creative Arts, Interlochen, Michigan, and am indebted to Artistic Director Katey Schultz. Katey has mentored me through individual consultations and monthly group sessions. Other Interlochen faculty members who gave their best advice include Michigan authors Anne Marie-Oomen, Mardi Jo Link, and Desiree Cooper. Also, publicist Ann Boland has provided not only useful information but, more importantly, the warmth of her friendship.

Visions to Reality: Charlotte Writer's Group critiqued many parts of this book. I am grateful to one member in particular, Margaret Krusinga, who helped with initial editing and structure. She gave good suggestions and made the book stronger with a better flow. Also, the Santa Cruz Chapter of the Society of Southwestern Authors became a critique group during my winters in Tuscon, Arizona. In particular, Mary Darling and Suzie Sarkozy read many of the complete stories and made valuable input, and Duke Southard gave me much encouragement.

The cover and photos in this book are a tribute to a photographer and graphic design couple in my hometown of Charlotte, Rod and Suzette Weaver. When the photos and cover began to take shape, it was thrilling. They helped make this project so much more attractive and professional. I am indebted to them. Finally, the entire Wheatmark team made the publication process seamless and without stress.

PREFACE

I wish I knew how it all started—this love of and curiosity for people whose lives are different from mine. My embrace has included people of other racial, socioeconomic, religious, and ethnic groups.

For all I know, it could have started in third grade at Taft School when Lynn Hanley, a new student from England with funny clothes, joined our class. In the beginning, she walked alone past my house to school; kids at school made fun of her because she wore long dresses, the type worn by girls in England and sent by her English aunts who believed this was what girls in America wore too. Lynn's hair was pulled back in tight braids, she wore brown Oxford shoes, and she had a thick British accent. One day I grabbed her hand, walked to school with her, and she became my friend.

Or, perhaps it started in Mr. Hansen's fifth-grade class, when we started a pen pal program with Japanese students. I remember the thrill of having a pen pal from the exotic country of Japan, compliments of an international exchange or goodwill program. It was the early 1950s, and as I reflect on the program today, it was, perhaps, an effort by education officials to diminish ill will toward the Japanese post-WWII. My father, who was stationed in Japan after the war, may have harbored ill will toward the country and its people—but his daughter did not.

I remember her name: Mitsuyu Yanome. The first letter I received came in a blue, onion-skin envelope. Details of the letter escape me, but

I'm sure they would have included basic stuff like, What do you like to do? What are your favorite subjects? How many brothers and sisters do you have?

Simply the thought that I was holding in my hand a letter written by someone in a distant part of the world took my breath away. And then, the best part—the gift exchange. I don't remember the gift I sent to Matsuyu, but I certainly remember what I received from her—a kimona. It was made of silk, pink with small flowers, and had a wide sash to wrap around my waist—a thing of beauty.

In my adult life, this fifth-grade pen pal exchange moved to the next level. I continued my interest in all things Japanese, including Japanese students who were part of a college exchange program. Two students stayed with me, and I remember being amused by the fact that the first word they looked up in their Japanese-to-English dictionary was "scale." They wanted to know how much weight they had gained from eating American hamburgers.

After high school, I moved into a Detroit inner-city neighborhood near Wayne State University's campus, and another new world unfolded. I had never been in the presence of so many African Americans. True to form, I relished learning about their family history of migrating from the South, bringing their own foods and culture with them.

These early years with people different from me in substantive ways sparked an interest and passion that never left. Unbeknownst to me then, these events would take me on a journey through different neighborhoods, towns, states, and countries where I could satisfy my intrigue.

Decades later, I would be sitting with each of eight women, recording their life stories to share with readers, who might find their varied lives of interest too.

INTRODUCTION TO ORDINARY WOMEN

Between 1980 and 2015, my work and subsequent retirement took me from Detroit to small Midwest towns and Tucson, Arizona. A solo traveler most of my adult life, I have made friends with and spent more time around women—from all walks of life. This book is about eight of them.

At first glance, none of the women may draw attention. But upon further reflection, I realized their lives are uncommon, either having defining moments not experienced by others, or living in a manner most do not. As a group, their lives encompass themes of immigration and assimilation, inner-city versus rural living, race, gender, age, religion, and rootedness in place and vocation. They range in age from sixty to ninety-eight.

Two of the women, Ina Zeemering and Jayne Jaffe Jordan, are World War II refugees. Their stories are some of the last to be told about a transformative transatlantic journey from rubble and despair to hope for a better life.

Sheila Kersey Harris, a black Canadian, crossed a body of water, too—only this one is two and a half miles shore to shore. She emigrated from small town Windsor, Ontario, crossing the Detroit River to the city of Detroit for work and marriage. While the border crossing suited her, it would not suit one of her daughters.

Carol Harton and Billie Qualtrough lived in an unsustainable and unhealthy environment. Carol's childhood was filled with violence and mental illness, and while Billie's childhood was happy, her Mormon marriage sucked the life blood from her. Both walked away—neither looked back.

Alice Barlass and Gladys Deland continue to find solace in the soil, producing food and feeding animals. Alice, eighty-seven, from Janesville, Wisconsin, and Gladys, ninety-seven, from Bellevue, Michigan, stay close to their roots, within miles of where they were raised. Neither ever felt the need to be anywhere else. Alice's seventy-year history in the Jersey cow industry is renowned.

Becoming rooted in a culture different from her own describes Constance Fletcher's life. For twenty-eight years, she served the Menominee Indian Reservation in Wisconsin, teaching vocals in a culture that honors drumming. But her greatest contribution may be the transformation of her students.

A brief introduction about how I met these women, as well as a few personal reflections where their themes touch my life, have been added. Historical contexts are included, where appropriate, to place each woman's life story in perspective.

Here, then, are eight ordinary women with lives most unusual.

PART I

CROSSING OCEANS AND RIVERS

AN INTRODUCTION: TWO IMMIGRANTS

Both are WWII refugees to the United States who emigrated, one from England in 1948, the other from the Netherlands in 1951. On the surface, this appears the sum total of their similarities. Jayne Jordan is tall, thin, and statuesque, with short hair of gray curls and waves. Ina Zeemering is of average height, with white permed hair and a few locks of blonde turned up at the edges.

Their faces are lined and occasionally display a stern look that belies a kind heart. Ina, seventy-five, has deep lines and scars, some the result of several surgeries after a serious auto accident, others from decades of sun exposure from working outside. For Jayne, eighty-seven, the lines signify more age-appropriate wrinkles.

Four hundred miles of Midwest road separates them now, and disparate economic circumstances separated them in their early lives. Ina remembers being poor when her family arrived in the United States, feeling shame in wearing hand-me-down clothes. Jayne was reared in a middle-class home on the Isle of Jersey and continued a middle-class lifestyle when she arrived here.

But uncanny similarities exist. A closer look at their life trajectories reveals that they both pursued paths toward financial independence, walking down roads where no or few women had tread, and they both read the *Wall Street Journal* daily.

Here in America they started their new lives from scratch. Their histories and stories follow.

_ 1 _

JAYNE JAFFE JORDAN

Photo Credit: Author

MEETING JAYNE

In September 2014, I met Jayne Jaffee Jordan in Lake Geneva, Wisconsin, at a book event sponsored by the American Association of University Women called "Soups and Signings." She was tall and thin with wavy gray hair and piercing blue eyes and accompanied by her daughter Lynne. We shared a six-foot author table. Jayne is of regal stature and walks like a woman who is in complete control, yet she expresses great doubt about her place here at this event. "I'm not the author—Jon should be here," she said.

When Jayne turned eighty, her daughter and son asked their friend Jon Helminiak to write Jayne's story to preserve the record of her wartime journey for future generations. It was to be a simple piece, Jayne believed, mostly for the perusal of her grandchildren. The 139-page book, *This Token of Freedom: A Remarkable Wartime Journey*, recounts Jayne's life from the Isle of Jersey in the English Channel to the United States during World War II and immediately thereafter.

Jayne was a reluctant participant at this book event, but her daughter persuaded her to come. Each of the authors was to be interviewed and answer questions about their book. Except Jayne—not the author but the subject of the book—was both unaccustomed to talking about herself and knew there were things she couldn't answer because she simply did not remember that far back. It didn't matter—the audience was entranced.

Jayne is eighty-seven now, has been in this country over sixty years, and still finds this interest in her life puzzling. But she is being profiled here because she is someone whose life was transformed by world events in a way most lives are not.

JAYNE JAFFE JORDAN:
AN IMMIGRANT'S LIFE

Since 2012, a distinctive piece of décor has graced the front façade of this tan brick colonial house on a tree-lined street in Whitefish Bay, Wisconsin. Two potted yellow mum plants complete the picture.

This 16" x 10" black-lacquered heavy iron oval-shaped plaque, with white lettering reading "The Myrtles" on the top and "J. H. Jaffe" on the bottom, has a tan Jersey cow placed prominently in the middle. In Jayne Jaffe's town on the Isle of Jersey, homes had names, not numbers. This symbol of the home of her birth took months to make its way from the Isle of Jersey in the English Channel to this Wisconsin home—a symbol of the fifty-year occupant's life journey.

Jayne's Early Life

Jayne Jaffe's life on the Isle of Jersey began on November 15, 1930. The Isle of Jersey is the farthest southern island of the Channel Islands in the English Channel and the largest. It is the closest British territory to Germany and twelve nautical miles from Normandy, France, facts that sealed its fate during World War II.

Jayne lived an idyllic life for nine years in rural Pontac Parish, ten miles from the capitol of St. Helier. She attended private school and, being an only child, was included in most of her parents' activities. She remembers cows grazing in the fields across from her house—Jersey cows—the namesake of the island. The cows are small, varying shades of brown and tan, have a white ring around their nose, and produce a distinctive milk rich with a layer of cream. A registry of this pure breed, the Herd Book, began in 1866 and is kept by the Royal Society of Agriculture and Horticulture.

Two life-changing events in Jayne's life occurred in 1939. Her father died unexpectedly at the age of fifty-seven, and the sounds of war grew louder and closer. On September 1, 1939, the Nazis invaded Poland, and their march into other countries began. The Channel Islands were not going to be defended by the British government, a strategic decision resulting in certain invasion. Jayne and her mother, Maureen, left the Isle of Jersey in 1939, only three weeks before Germany invaded the Island. Eighty percent of the population did not leave. Jayne and her mother went to live with her maternal aunt, originally in Brighton and then in London. But Jayne's safety could not be secured here, either.

Jayne embraced Aunt Adj, her "fun auntie," and the moves to Brighton and London with a sense of adventure. Adj was single, sang opera, and travelled. She was an independent spirit, and Jayne was smitten with her lifestyle. Further, Jayne had read about London in school and was excited to be going there. Jayne's mother remained upbeat about the moves, not revealing any sense of danger. But, Jayne would not be staying in England for long as the bombs were coming. She would be coming to America.

Jayne's Evacuation

Five million American families were willing to welcome children from England preceding the bombing. Businesses in America offered to financially help those families who could not afford transport, one being the *Boston Evening Transcript* newspaper. Through these contributions, five hundred British children sailed out of harm's way via Boston. Jayne was one of them.

On August 10, 1940, nine-year-old Jayne and her mother arrived at the Grosvenor Home Hotel in London, where Jayne would say goodbye. Although neither knew it, they would not see each other again for five years. Jayne boarded a bus that would take her to Liverpool, and then boarded the SS *Samaria*, which would take her to the United States and into the custody of the United States Committee for the Care of European Children.

Many of the children who boarded the ship, including Jayne, saw this as an adventure. She was sad to be leaving her mother and Aunt Adj, but she was not afraid. Maureen had raised her daughter to be self-reliant. "There was never a time when I was timid," Jayne said. But also, the thinking at the time was that this separation would not last long.

Jayne's ship made it safely to New York. But, unbeknownst to Jayne and her mother, this journey to the United States was fraught with peril. Previously, the ships carrying evacuees were escorted by battleships. But many escort ships had been torpedoed, fewer ships were available, and those were needed to protect the homeland's shore from invasion.

Thus, Jayne's ship and a few thereafter were not provided the same protection as others. In fact, on September 18, 1940, three weeks after Jayne's arrival to her final destination in Wisconsin, another ship, the *City of Benares*, was torpedoed and sunk, taking seventy-seven children with it. This event effectively ended the program to evacuate children by sea.

Welcome to America

Jayne's life in the United States began with the Sullivan family in Fox Point, Wisconsin, a middle-class northern Milwaukee suburb. Willis Sullivan was a lawyer, his wife, Helen, a homemaker, and there were two sons, Bob and Bill, one of whom was Jayne's age. Although it's not clear that the Sullivan boys were thrilled to have her in their home, they did their best to make her feel welcome. Jayne knew that, in the beginning, she got all of the attention and could tell they were not happy. She tried not to do anything to make their jealousy worse.

Jayne's adjustments were those of any immigrant child. She spoke English but was teased mercilessly at school because of her British accent. She quickly determined it had to go.

Mrs. Sullivan served as a surrogate mother and made sure Jayne had the same clothes as other girls. Although she was not as outgoing, warm, and demonstrative as Jayne's mother, she became the closest adult woman in Jayne's life, and Jayne was treated as a member of the family.

"Mrs. Sullivan treated me like a daughter, and this meant doing dishes and other housework," Jayne said.

"Her friends thought it was wrong for her to have me do dishes and other housework, but I didn't," Jayne said. She didn't want any special treatment.

Much of Jayne's American life was indistinguishable from that of American girls. She made friends with other girls, went shopping, went on vacation to the Sullivans' northern cabin, and became Americanized in dress and manner. The war in Europe continued, and Jayne's life was unaffected by it—until December 7, 1941.

On that day, she was staying at a girlfriend's home when the Sullivans were away and remembers her friend's parents listening closely to the radio when they heard that Pearl Harbor was bombed.

"You could tell the news was shocking and very upsetting to the adults," she said. Jayne knew that the president had resisted getting the United States involved in the war and, although she did not yet understand the implications of this, she knew the worst had happened.

Pearl Harbor had been bombed by the Japanese—Franklin Roosevelt had declared war. For three and a half more years, Jayne stayed with the Sullivans—until it was time for her to go home in September 1945.

Conditions Back Home

Author Julie Summers wrote *When the Children Came Home: Stories of Wartime Evacuees,* using interviews and memoirs to tell personal stories that created a portrait of wartime Britain and the homecoming of the children. One of the Australian evacuees interviewed expressed the following sentiment: "They (parents) had to accept the person I had become. Looking back on it now, I find it sad to think how hard that must have been for them, losing me as a little girl and getting back a headstrong adolescent who knew her mind and did not want to be told."

Jayne expressed it this way—"I was a pain in the neck when I got home."

The postwar conditions were harsh. "People thought we had rationing in the United States, but, that's a joke. It was 1945 and a mess in England," she said.

Her transition back home was not smooth. She had lost her British accent and was treated cruelly by other teenagers as a "Yank." She admits she was totally American, including wearing slacks, which was seen as scandalous and inappropriate for young women. She convinced her mother that they needed to return to the United States.

"I'm coming home." –Jayne

On April 15, 1948, with the help of Willis Sullivan, seventeen-year-old Jayne and Maureen Jaffe made their way back to the Milwaukee area. They were some of the 205,000 refugees to come to the United States after the war between 1946 and 1952. Maureen was trying desperately to hold onto her daughter. The war had taken the British daughter she had known and transformed her into a full-blown American young woman—one who no longer needed her mother's guidance. She had become her own person.

While Maureen and Jayne lived, worked, and enjoyed time together over the next two years, Maureen was never comfortable in the United States. America was not her home, plus, she felt Americans had little sensitivity to the difference in loss and destruction the war had wrought in England compared to the United States.

Jayne, on the other hand, felt totally at home in Milwaukee, back among her friends, and did not have her mother's sensitivities about the war because she had not experienced the losses. When Maureen wanted to move to Hollywood, where she had a distant relative, Jayne went along, hoping her mother would be more comfortable. But Hollywood, especially, had all the latest post-war movies about the United States coming in to save the day in the war. Only years later did Jayne understand the total lack of regard shown for the losses and hardships incurred by the British.

In the fall of 1949, Maureen returned to the Isle of Jersey. While her homestead was gone, having disappeared during the German occupation, Maureen still had friends in the capitol city of St. Helier. It would be the first time in many years that she would be content. For five years, she lived a good life, returning to the United States for Jayne's wedding and to meet her first grandchild. Not long after her last trip, after having lunch with friends, she went home, laid down, and never woke up. She was fifty-four.

Jayne Begins Her Adult Life

A short time after Maureen returned to Jersey, Jayne returned to Milwaukee and went to a summer party with her friends. There she met Rich Jordan, a son of the head of the Better Business Bureau in the area. She was nineteen when they married. Jayne was excited about becoming a mother, and two children, Lynne and Michael, were born of the union.

The Jordans, Jayne's in-laws, lived in Tucson, and Jayne and Rich lived there for the first few years of their marriage. They moved back to the Milwaukee area, and Jayne then began the process of pursuing her ultimate goal—becoming a citizen of the United States. But first she had to study for the test that asked about her knowledge of the Constitution (ten questions). She already met the other requirements of being able to speak and understand English.

In the massive granite Federal Building on Knapp Street in downtown Milwaukee sits the US Citizenship and Immigration Office. In 1955, Jayne went for her exam, taking Willis Sullivan, her friend and a lawyer, with her, figuring if there was any trouble, he could help. When they arrived in the right room, Bill sat at the back while Jayne approached the front and sat across the table from the immigration official.

"There were long tables with immigration officials on one side and maybe thirty people on the other. I might have been the only one with an American accent. The officials were mean to the others, and I felt sorry for them. At one point, my official said, 'You were supposed to reapply for admission to the country and report every year.'

"The guy started threatened me, saying, 'This could send you to jail.'

"Willis Sullivan came to the table because he had heard what the guy said. 'Is there a problem here?' he asked. With his intervention, I was able to become a citizen."

Family

Jayne was twenty-five when her mother died, but she continued to have another adult woman in her life—Helen Sullivan. Even though the Sullivans divorced in the early 1950s, Helen remained a good friend to Jayne, was present during Christmas holidays, and served as a surrogate grandmother to Jayne's children. Her own grandchildren were like cousins to Jayne's son and daughter.

Jayne knew this relationship with two generations of her host family was special because she had met a few other evacuees.

"I knew that their families were not anywhere as close as I was with the Sullivans," she said.

But Jayne missed her mother and father in one respect—their warmth.

"The Sullivans were not a warm family," she said. She raised her children much as she had been raised. "My daughter Lynne and her boys are very warm and close. Now, my son Mike is like Lynne. Some men are and some aren't."

In 1967, when Jayne was thirty-seven, her marriage of seventeen years ended. Her husband came to her one day and said, "I'm leaving." Jayne was stunned. Not only was he leaving her and the children, he was moving to Arizona.

As the story unfolded, it appeared that Rich had been having an affair with a former neighbor, which started a few years earlier. When the neighbor's husband died, she moved to Arizona. Around the same time, Jayne's family moved to Whitefish Bay and had been living there for two years.

But the relationship between Rich and the former neighbor continued in some form and fashion unbeknownst to Jayne. When she looked back, trying to identify the clues she may have missed, she remembered one thing her former neighbor's husband said one day in the backyard before he died.

"Don't you know what's going on?" he asked. She didn't know what he was talking about.

Rich was going to join the former neighbor and her children in Arizona. He had been an entrepreneur and a builder. He had wonderful ideas and, in fact, had built a lovely local shopping center. But it appeared he overspent. When he left town, there was no money to be had. Jayne did not contact an attorney until creditors started arriving at the front door wanting to be paid for his debts.

"I was left high and dry."

Jayne became a single mother with secretarial skills looking for work. Secretarial work was not going to allow her to keep the same standard of living.

"I was very worried about money. I wanted to keep everything as it had been for the children's sake. I was fortunate to still receive a small dividend check from the company that purchased my father's company on the Isle of Jersey. I was able to use that to pay the mortgage. Plus, there was a little money in savings. The first six months were difficult."

Yet, his parents were a constant presence in the children's lives, and she was bound and determined not to alienate the children from their father. They continued to have a relationship through regular telephone conversations and summer visits with him and his eventual wife. When that marriage ended in divorce, he married again. He is now deceased.

Employment and a Rorschach Test

Jayne was fortunate to have contacts with people in the financial services industry through her leadership in the Junior League, a philanthropic organization of women supporting the arts. People were aware of her financial situation, with no child support.

One of her male friends ran an office downtown and asked her to come and talk to him.

He said he wanted to hire her as an office manager. She surveyed the situation.

"What you need is a housemother, and I'm not interested." He said, 'I knew you wouldn't want to do this. I want you to become a stockbroker.'"

She had lunch with another male friend in financial services after that and told him about the previous conversation. "He walked across the street to his office and said to the broker, 'You need to hire this person.'"

As it turned out, there was an opening—but first she had to be approved by an industrial psychologist, Dr. Hummer. Jayne would come face to face with the Rorschach test, named after Swiss psychologist Hermann Rorschach. In the 1960s, this test was the most widely used projective process by which people responded to ambiguous stimuli.

Subjects' perceptions of inkblots are recorded and then analyzed using psychological interpretation. Employers use this test to examine a person's personality characteristics and emotional functioning. Jayne couldn't fathom the value of such a test. She thought it was ridiculous.

"I thought it was awful! I was shocked they gave me the job. Dr. Hummer said I was a good candidate. I guessed he figured out things I couldn't see."

Studying for the Stockbroker Test

Jayne began working in the office and underwent on-the-job training at various offices. There was one woman broker in the downtown office, and Jayne was sent to sit next to her and listen to her conversations with clients. Then, she began studying to become a licensed stockbroker by taking the Uniform Securities Agents State Law Exam and the General Securities Registered Representative Exam. The tests are known for their rigor.

"I had to study a lot before I took the test. Each aspect of financial services was tested separately. I studied when the kids were not home and after they went to bed."

No other women took the test on any of the days she sat. She took each section of the test over a period of time and passed all of them. The year was 1968, and women were just beginning to get into the field; Jayne met, and to her knowledge, shadowed the only other female stockbroker in the state of Wisconsin.

"I was a pioneer female stockbroker. Every radio program, even Jack LeLanne, when he came to town, I was on that TV show. Newspapers wrote articles—it was a big deal." She was written up in many newspapers.

"I think some men see women differently, but very seldom did I have a problem. Only on one day when I took cold calls, a man thought he was talking to a man because I have a deep voice. He asked me my name. When I told him it was Jayne, he said, 'Oh you are a woman.' I said, if that's a problem, I'll transfer you. It was and I did."

"It turned out to be an advantage for me with women customers. A lot of women were much more comfortable talking to me. Many men had kept their wives in the dark; women knew nothing about stocks and securities. I was more patient explaining things to them."

"But I had more men than women clients. There may have been some men employed in the field who did not welcome women, but when that happened, I felt I had been through enough, and I was not about to be intimidated. I enjoyed it for thirty-three and a half years, and I retired when I was seventy. I liked what I did and didn't see any need to retire any earlier."

The Stockbroker Becomes a Shareholder

Jayne, like most Wisconsinites, became a rabid fan of the NFL team, the Green Bay Packers. Her husband went to school in Green Bay, and they went to as many games as possible. When her marriage ended, her love for the team did not. "Even today, I don't like any distractions when I watch the game."

The Packers, unlike all other NFL teams, are owned by everyday people as shareholders, not one owner. While not a typical ownership arrangement with shareholder rights and voting, there is an annual shareholder meeting held at Lambeau Stadium.

In 1997, the franchise needed to sell more shares to raise money for improvements at the stadium. So, when they issued a call for buyers of 100,000 more shares, and 105,989 new shareholders answered the call, Jayne was one of them. Unbeknownst to her, so was her son.

There are currently over five million shares outstanding and approximately 364,114 owners. "You should see what the annual meetings are like, with babies in Packer outfits, and, of course, cheeseheads. It's a sight to behold."

Winding Down—Patron of the Arts

Jayne's love of music began when she was a girl; she attended many concerts over fifty years. "I always loved music and became a spectator early in my life," she said. When she joined the Junior League in her thirties, she participated in fundraising for the arts. She became president of the organization and contributed her time and resources to improving the arts in the Milwaukee area.

Not long after she retired, she attended a Women's Club luncheon where they discussed the need for new facilities for the Milwaukee Youth Symphony Orchestra (MYSO). Their then-current space was too cramped for practice and recitals. "I got involved right away on a fund-raising effort for the Old Schlitz Garage," she said. She also became chair of the MYSO.

The Jordans—Generation Two—Paying it Forward

Just as the second generation of Sullivans continued their support for immigrant-turned-US-citizen Jayne Jaffe Jordan, so a second generation of Jordans would pay it forward by supporting future generations too.

Jayne's son, Mike Jordan, upon retirement, replaced Jayne as chair of MYSO. The focus of this group's efforts was to expand musical training access to a broader community, particularly the impoverished youth of southeastern Milwaukee and northern Illinois.

In fact, in 2016 at the White House, First Lady Michelle Obama gave an award to MYSO for its unique musical outreach to those children in neighborhoods that would not normally have these opportunities to learn and display their creativity and talent.

At the homestead in Whitefish Point, Jayne, at the age of eighty-seven, still mows her own lawn under the watchful eyes of her newer neighbors, who are in awe of her fifty-year residency. While many of her friends have either died or are in senior centers, she's not so sure she could make the adjustment. She keeps her mind and body active by playing Bridge and golf, attending plays and concerts, and making an annual trip to Las Vegas with her friends.

Little evidence exists in this home of Jayne's British birth—except a framed painting on the south living room wall. The 11" x 15" painting of a British flag is the only in-house reminder that Jayne was an immigrant to this country. The artist and friend, Maureen Coffey, wanted Jayne to have this piece, a dual symbol of her heritage and her love of the arts.

A strong woman who refused to be intimidated, a son who took up the mantel of his mother in exposing more Milwaukee children to the arts, and an untold number of beneficiaries—some might suggest this a most unusual track record for an ordinary World War II immigrant.

2

INA ZEEMERING

Photo Credit: Rod Weaver

HISTORICAL CONTEXT
The Hongerwinter: Dutch Famine (1944-45)

The year she was born, there was food for her family. Fifteen months later, famine weighed on them like a dark cloud. It would not lift until the Allied troops liberated their country—the Netherlands—in May 1945.

Ina Zeemering was born in an eastern province in the Netherlands in 1943, midway through WWII. Following the German invasion, all Dutch families used food ration coupons that provided barely sufficient caloric intake for adults and children. In September 1944, the situation worsened.

Not only was food in shorter supply, so was fuel. A serious shortage of fuel caused a gradual decrease and eventual shutdown of the production of gas and electricity—stoves and furnaces could no longer be used.

In some places, water had to be cut off. The situation was dire: no gas, no electricity, no light or heat, and no clean water. Laundries ceased operating as soap for personal use was unavailable. In addition, large quantities of food and cattle were siphoned off for German troops.

People stood in line for hours at soup kitchens set up by private organizations to provide one meal a day. Children were given priority for food, consisting of beans and rice. The second priority for food allotments was those who presented medically necessary cases, defined as adults who were 30 percent below the average weight for their age and gender. The ration coupons, which originally provided 1,500 calories per day, eventually decreased to five to six hundred—bordering on starvation intake.

The Perfect Storm: Famine Conditions

Several factors contributed to the famine that consumed the country for eight months.

In September of 1944, the exiled Dutch government appealed to their Dutch countrymen for a railway strike to further support the Allied liberation. In retaliation, the German administration in the country placed an embargo on all food transports. In November, the embargo was partially lifted, but food transports across water ceased.

The war was turning against the Germans. They bombed bridges across the Rhine in an effort to impede Allied advances from the South. In November an early, harsh winter froze the canals that had previously been used by barges to ship in flour for bread. People were forced to eat tulip bulbs and sugar beets. In late 1944, children were transported to rural areas of the country where there were farms with produce and milk.

In April 1945, the Allies were able to negotiate with the Germans to allow for food drops in exchange for a cessation of bombing German positions. In efforts called Operations Manna and Chowhound, the Royal Air Force and the Royal Canadian Air Force dropped food from April 29 to May 7, 1945, in Operation Manna, and the United States Army Air Force dropped food between May 1 and May 8, 1945 in Operation Chowhound.

The Legacy of Famine

During the famine, infant mortality rose dramatically. Immediately thereafter, doctors saw increased cases of tuberculosis and typhoid fever caused by the unhealthy conditions people were forced to live in due to lack of fuel, soap, disinfectant, and water. Six weeks after liberation, doctors were presiding over thousands of patients in the throes of starvation. It is estimated that between 18,000 and 22,000 deaths could be attributed to malnutrition.

Ina's brother, Fritz, eight and a half years old in 1945, would not escape the trauma of the famine or starvation—he became malnourished. Immediately after the War, he was sent by the International Committee of the Red Cross to a hospital in Switzerland, where he stayed for months.

Ina was too young to remember any of these events. The timing of her birth was fortuitous, because until the day they died, all of Ina's immediate family members remembered the hunger.

INA ZEEMERING:
A DIFFERENT KIND OF HUNGER

In the end, all you have is your intellect and your talent. —Ina Zeemering

The Netherlands during WWII

They didn't believe that Hitler would do it. The Dutch believed if their country claimed neutrality during this war, as they had in WWI, it would be enough to save them. Hadn't the Netherlands sheltered the German Kaiser after WWI, allowing him to live there in exile? Surely, these two things would protect them.

Ina Zeemering's father, Garrit, was one who did not see the invasion coming. But come it did on September 1, 1939, when the Germans attacked the Dutch merchant fleet. After three days of fighting, the Dutch surrendered.

Prior to the war, Ina's father had been a police officer and then in the Dutch military; after the German invasion, the nature of his work was murkier. Ina's mother, Katerina, would only see him sporadically, and she did not know where he was for long periods of time. This is the environment into which Ina Zeemering was born on June 14, 1943, in a small town in the eastern province of Overijssel.

An Idyllic Childhood

Ina's earliest memories are of a childhood surrounded by fields. The family included her mother, Katerina, her brother, Fritz (six and a half years older), and her sister, Gerda (nine years older). Ina's father, Garrit, was not in her life for the first two years, but her paternal grandparents were; they owned a dairy farm several miles away, a source of milk for the family, and the location of the large extended family gathering of Zeemerings for the annual family vacation.

Across the road from the house stood a blackberry thicket and fields of rutabagas and potatoes. The family struggled to have nutritious meals. Ina has only one memory of food:

"After the War, I remember getting an orange for Christmas."

Ina's mother worried constantly about being able to feed her family. For thirty years after the war she suffered, waking up with nightmares of not having food to feed her children. This is why she refused to discuss the war with Ina—the memories were emotionally crushing. She would share only one memory related to food:

"My mother said she and my father rode their bicycles miles to my grandparents' farm to get milk for me when I was young. That is the reason I have good teeth," Ina said.

Ina has fond memories of a happy childhood, playing in the fields across from her home with her German Shepherd, Kazan. The two had grown up together. Her home was on the property of the military academy, now the site of the Netherlands National Police Academy. When Ina's father came home from the war, he taught at the Netherlands National Police Training Centre.

Ina's mother was traumatized by the War, and her father's family had memories filled with horror as well. His older brother had been a member of the Dutch Underground and was captured by the Germans. His torture consisted of having all of his nails pulled out and all of his fingers and toes broken. He then had to dig his own grave and was summarily shot in the Town Square—three days before the Armistice.

Ina's parents decided to leave these memories behind, putting distance between themselves and the past. So they requested visas to leave the Netherlands and enter Canada or the United States. Ina's father had to petition his government employer for an early retirement after twenty-two years of service because of Katerina's delicate emotional condition and his son's fragile physical condition.

They planned to immigrate to Canada to farm, but the visa for the United States came through one day before they were to leave for Canada. They were sponsored by Garrit's former colleague, one of many, who had immigrated earlier to Grand Rapids, Michigan.

Emigration Day

Ina keeps a photo of the day they left their home to come to the United States:

"I wore a new jacket, a bow in my hair, and I carried my doll."

Then, her parents told her the dog would not be coming.

"I remember weeping profusely. I was inconsolable. As the car was driving away, my last memory is looking out the back window of our car at the neighbor sitting on the stoop with my dog.

"Such a terrible thing to do to a little girl. Many years later I cried when I recalled his incident. It's probably why I have owned mostly German Shepherd dogs all my life."

A Meager Life in Grand Rapids

Not unlike other immigrants, the first Zeemering family home in Grand Rapids was an apartment above a store in the downtown area. Garrit got a job working for a residential painter. Sometimes, he didn't get paid.

Ina attended public school the first year.

"I was seven years old, in second grade, and knew no English.

"We were in a lower middle-class neighborhood where you could play in the street.

"My first friend was black."

In third grade, Ina transferred to a private Christian school. "I suspect I left the public school because it was largely black. But my mother always said it was because I needed tutoring in order to catch up with my classes, and the public schools could not provide this."

Private education was a financial hardship because of tuition. By this time, Garrit had gone into business for himself as a residential painter.

"I used to help him when I was small. On weekends, I would go with him to homes where he painted. I would pick up scraps off the floor and pull nails out of the drywall."

Money was always tight. "I remember my mother put money in envelopes in a shoe box, one for rent, one for the car, one for food, utilities, etc."

"There was one time my dad didn't get paid from a customer. My mother said he was being too kind to people. I didn't see the value in that. I said, 'He's stupid.' In retrospect, I see it was unkind of me to say that. I just remember having very little money, especially after I started at the Christian school."

In elementary school, Ina's primary memory is that the other students were much wealthier than she—while she had to wear hand-me-down clothes. She was embarrassed, and her self-esteem suffered.

Then, there were other costs associated with being in a middle-class school, such as the cost of renting musical instruments. Ina took up guitar and joined a chorale group.

"I recall having conversations with my parents about money, or the lack of it, more than once a week."

Assimilation of the Dutch Girl

Ina was a quick study, both academically and in learning to fit in with kids who were the children of doctors and lawyers. With the help of a tutor, she learned to speak English quickly. She loved music, song, and sports. In high school, she really shined.

"I loved basketball, and sports and music were my way to fit into a particular clique.

"My high school music teacher singled me out for being the best alto at school.

"Looking back, there was a lack of self-esteem, and the only thing I had was my talent and my intellect; I had to prove to myself that I was as good as the other kids were."

Being Driven: Work Ethic and Family Support

At the age of fourteen, Ina got a job at a fruit farm, picking peaches and cherries. In addition, she babysat, worked at a car wash, and eventually cashiered at Meijer Thrifty Acres.

"I always drove myself because I thought I was going to be seen as lazy and slovenly if I didn't."

In her junior and senior years of high school, she paid her own private school tuition in the amount of $345, paid for a trip to Amsterdam, and gave a loan to her sister in the amount of $500 for a down payment on a new house.

Over time, Ina's parents moved to other houses, fixing them up, and moving on. But they never achieved any degree of financial stability. Later in life, Ina would help them purchase three acres of land to live on in retirement in Carmen, Arizona. After Ina's dad died, her mother lived in a trailer on the property until her eightieth birthday.

College, Loves, and Loss

Ina was a stellar student and had no trouble getting admitted to the University of Michigan in Ann Arbor, Michigan, where she majored in political science—and met her first real love, Russ Penning. Russ was the best friend of her first boyfriend who had rejected her. He studied Engineering, and she and Russ remained an item not only during under-graduate school but into Ina's master's degree program at Wayne State University in Detroit.

But there were signs of trouble early on.

"Russ did not want any children and wanted to live in a rural environment in northern Michigan after graduation. He did not want me to get a PhD after I got my master's degree—not wanting his wife to have more education than he did."

"My sister kept telling me, 'Quit beating him at tennis because he's not going to marry you.' I couldn't understand why I couldn't be me and still have this man."

The relationship ended. He wanted to get back together a few years later, but by that time, she had moved on.

Mother-Daughter Relationship

Russ Penning was not the only person in Ina's life to try to tamp down her ambition. Ina had a conflicted relationship with her mother. Perhaps, because of Katarina's wartime experiences fraught with peril and fear, she was unable to show love, becoming emotionally distant.

One conversation stays with Ina that illustrates her mother's aloofness. One Saturday morning her mother called, after a friend of Ina's had died unexpectedly. Ina was grief-stricken.

"You sound low," Katerina said.

"My friend, David Serotkin, dropped dead unexpectedly."

"That's what happens when you get older," Katarina responded.

Ina had expected more empathy from her mother, and she got a chance to tell her so years later. When she did, her mother teared up.

"Don't ever think I don't care. I just can't express my words like you can," Katerina said.

But there was one strong verbal message she did manage to convey to Ina: *Don't fly too high*. Ina's father's message, on the other hand, was that there wasn't anything Ina couldn't do. Ina believed him, achieving one academic and financial success after another.

Pushing the Envelope and Becoming 'A First'

In 1963, during Ina's sophomore year at University of Michigan, Gerald Ford was the chair of the House Republican Conference in Congress during the Kennedy administration. She applied to go to Washington, DC for six weeks that summer to be an intern in Ford's office. She was accepted, the first and only female in Ford's office, along with men whose names we would come to know: Donald Rumsfeld, Jack Kemp, and John Lindsey.

"Gerald Ford was just a good guy. He was a decent human being, with an ordinary family," Ina said.

Later, when Ina was in her political science master's program at Wayne State University, she applied for a Gerald Ford Fellowship to work in the office of the speaker of the house in the Michigan legislature. It was the eighth year of the fellowship, and students from Michigan State, Wayne State, and University of Michigan applied, with a committee screening all of the applicants.

The committee member from Wayne State rejected her application outright, saying "They don't take women." Ina remembers going to her faculty advisor in a state of distress.

He said: "Ina, you are one of the most original thinkers I know. We are going to push your application."

Her application was approved, and she found herself again the only female intern, this time in the Michigan House of Representatives, assigned to the Democratic speaker of the house. But a serious auto accident in 1969 would derail her work there.

The Accident

What she remembers the most is that she never lost consciousness. She and one of the other Ford Fellows were in a Mustang, coming home from a get-together in East Lansing, driving west on Michigan Avenue, when they were broadsided on the passenger side by a pickup truck. Ina was sitting in the passenger seat and was hit by the silver frame from the small side window. It flew into her face right below her eyes.

"It was a miracle I didn't lose my eyesight. The impact threw us both into the median, but Rob barely got hurt. I remember the EMTs picking leaves out of my hair; there was so much blood, they just wrapped my head and took me to Sparrow Hospital.

"I was in the hospital for a while, and I had several surgeries. We had to sue to get the other driver's insurance company to pay anything. The driver was a young guy, and he didn't own anything of value. I had to pay for much of the medical treatment out of my pocket.

"Since then, I have always been self-conscious about my face."

Also, she lost her job in the Michigan legislature.

Law, Politics, Rejection, and 'Another First'

Entrance to law school requires taking the Law School Aptitude Test (LSAT). The test is a very intricate multiple-choice exam, with long passages to read, followed by multiple-choice answers that are remarkably similar. It has been criticized over time for being biased.

Ina struggled with this type of exam, not achieving a score high enough to be admitted to Wayne State University Law School. She had never had any academic failures or deficiencies and wrote to the admissions office, decrying their unwillingness to admit her in spite of her strong record of academic excellence.

She was admitted to the Detroit College of Law in 1970, when there were not many female students. Her graduating class in 1973 had five women out of 232 graduates. She encountered no problems with her studies; then, she learned that the diploma she was to receive at graduation had the words *conferring upon **him** a diploma.*

Ina again challenged the status quo, marching up the steps to the second floor to the dean's office to discuss the issue. Six months later, she became the first to receive a diploma that said the college *conferred upon the above-named person* a juris doctor degree. Starting in 1975, all future diplomas read *conferred upon the above-named person.* Her challenge was not well received by some students. The diploma had to be made slightly smaller to accommodate the additional words.

When Ina took the Michigan Bar Exam to be admitted to practice law in Michigan, her essay score was in the ninety-eighth percentile. She made sure to send a copy of this score to the dean of the law school that originally refused to admit her.

In 1978, Ina was appointed as a referee in the Traffic and Ordinance Division of Recorder's Court in Detroit. She took the bench in 1979. Her appointment was not welcomed by all, however. Another sitting judge whose family was building a dynasty in the judicial community saw that seat as "belonging" to his son, and he told her so. He told her to reject her appointment.

"I told him I wasn't going to do that. I liked the idea of sitting on the bench and saw this as a beginning of a judicial career."

She was on the bench for three years when a new district court system was created by the Michigan legislature, and all judges had to run in an election. Over ninety candidates filed their papers; Ina was not a finalist.

Buying Houses and Dreams of Land

Ina began practicing law and bought her first house when she was twenty-five. The small house on Homedale in Detroit was in a Polish-German immigrant community. Little did she know that acquiring this first piece of real estate would eventually allow her to realize her one true dream—owning land.

"I bought a house because I wanted to be sure I could have pets. I always had a cat and dog growing up, and some rental apartments would not allow pets."

"I spent a lot of time on weekends looking at farm property. I probably saw twenty pieces of property. I had a friend in mid-Michigan, and the land was cheap there; but, it was too far away. I was determined to buy property located no more than one hour from Detroit. This was where my center of operation was."

In 1979, she purchased an old three-story Victorian home on Canfield Street, south of the Wayne State University campus in Detroit. The house needed a lot of work; her plan was to live in one part and rent out the rest as apartment units. This was her first adventure as a landlord; being a lawyer would prove to come in handy. She continued to leverage more real estate purchases, thereby minimizing her tax obligations.

But in 1986, one incident would change her life. She awoke in the middle of the night to a sound. Actually, it was a man's voice in her bedroom. He had a gun to her head:

"Keep your dog quiet so I don't have to shoot him. If you remain calm, this will just be a robbery."

She was asked to get her jewelry and wallet, and she complied. She remained calm, and the man left. But the robbery would forever change her ability to feel safe in that home. Within two years, she would be gone.

Horses and Houses

As a young girl, Ina remembers seeing the movie *Wildfire* about a horse that died; she was grief-stricken. Then, at about the age of thirteen, she babysat for people who owned a Welch Pony, which she learned to ride.

"It's interesting how the forces in our lives attach to one another. When I was practicing law, I met someone who I went to graduate school with. We started talking about horses, and he said, 'Come and see our horses.' I did, and I was hooked. They helped me find my first horse. We went to Ontario, Canada, and saw a mare with her eight-week-old daughter (Sarrafina, an Egyptian Arabian). The clouds parted. I bought the horse for $18,000, half of which I borrowed.

"I remember sitting on the floor in the horse trailer, bringing her back to Michigan. Riding in a horse trailer with a horse is very dangerous—it just isn't done. I knew this. If she had been spooked by anything, she could have killed me."

Other horses would follow. At one point, Ina owned thirteen Egyptian Arabians. Some were leased, but it became clear early on that breeding and selling Egyptian Arabian horses could not support their own keep. Something else would have to support them.

A New Home

In 1988, on a spring weekend afternoon, a few pup tents could be seen along the south side of Mac Road, between Curdy and Argentine, in Oceola Township in south-central Michigan. The occupants were there to celebrate Ina's first land acquisition. Several women, who had brought sleeping bags and food, set up their pup tents and relaxed, enjoying the country day. When nightfall arrived, they got ready to hunker down for the night.

It was a beautiful setting, except for one thing. No large trees adorned the property, and the only structure on the land was an old, rundown barn—no outhouses. So the women had to take care of business in nature. They worried incessantly that the tent and their hygiene activities might be too close to the dirt road—with car headlights flashing them as they dropped their drawers. Fortunately, the area was still remote, only a few cars drove by, and they were saved from sure embarrassment.

Becoming a Builder

First there were a hundred acres, then 120. Over twenty-five years, land was perked; two barns and several houses went up on ten-acre lots. The barns would become training arenas for the horses.

Some days Ina can be found picking up scraps off the floors left by workers in her new houses, reminiscent of the work she did sixty-five years earlier with her father. Some days she can be seen cleaning and staining wood moldings in her newly built houses, all made from downed oak trees on her property. Or she might be seen riding her tractor lawn-mower on her remaining hundred acres.

But most days you can see her walking down her winding, dirt driveway to the barn with her German Shepherd Anya, preparing to feed the horses. Sometimes, she will clean the horse stalls or pitch hay, although as she ages, the hardest physical labor is increasingly done by others.

Horses are no longer bred, but houses are still being built—all with handicap accessibility. Now her thoughts turn to other things, such as returning to the Netherlands one last time.

Also, she is now finalizing work on the Zeemering Family and Human Therapy Foundation. The foundation will be the not-for-profit organization that owns the land preserve, using a conservation or devel-opmental easement allowed by Michigan law. It is Ina's way to assure that the remaining acreage with timberland will continue in its natural state in perpetuity, with support from her estate.

Conclusion: She Flew Too High

Ina's mother, Katerina, died in 1997. But during her lifetime, she spent many weeks at her daughter's horse ranch, marveling at all she had achieved. She found peace at the farm that had escaped her all her life.

"She always told me not to work so hard," Ina said.

Perhaps, in retrospect, Katerina was glad her daughter didn't follow her advice to *not fly too high*. In the end, she was proud of her immigrant daughter, who chose not to follow the typical path for women, regardless of criticism from many.

She preferred to travel her own journey and be her own person—living on the land, much like her Dutch ancestors.

— 3 —

SHEILA KERSEY HARRIS

Photo Credit: Author

MEETING SHEILA

In the early 1980s in Detroit, I met Sheila Rogers, a black Canadian who lived across the Detroit River in Windsor, Ontario, Canada. I had become a Detroit resident in the mid-1960s during my undergraduate college years at Wayne State University and remained for twenty-seven years for additional education and employment. During those years, I became friends with many African Americans. Sheila was the only black Canadian I met.

My father was born in Halifax, Nova Scotia, Canada in 1911. In 1928, he immigrated to Detroit with his mother to join his father, who had come earlier to find employment in the automotive industry. All Canadians I came to know throughout the first thirty-five years of my life were white relatives, who lived in the province of Ontario, bordering the Detroit River.

Blacks in Canada

When people think of Black Canadians, more often than not, they think of black people from any number of islands or Africa who have immigrated to Toronto, Canada, the city with the largest black population in the country. Generally, they do not think of blacks who have been in the country for more than one hundred and fifty years.

But having studied African-American History at Wayne State University, I knew that blacks, mostly slaves, but some freedmen, began arriving in Western or Upper Canada in the late 1700s, and more arrived after September of 1833 when slavery was abolished in all British lands. Between then and the Civil War, when even blacks in free states were in harm's way, greater numbers arrived.

Secreting fugitives across the Detroit River by boat, only 800 yards across in places, was the method used to move slaves to freedom. I assumed Sheila's ancestors came to what was at times called Upper and then Western Canada (now Ontario) in exactly this manner. I was only half right—Sheila's paternal ancestors, in all probability, came this way.

As Sheila and I became better acquainted, we talked about our respective family histories. I told her my father was born and raised in Nova Scotia, and I had first cousins in Windsor.

"Maybe our families were neighbors," she said.

"You mean in Windsor?" I asked.

"No, in Nova Scotia," she replied.

"My mother's family came from Nova Scotia," she stated.

I was stunned. I had no knowledge of any black presence in Nova Scotia in the early 1900s. Sheila said her mother's people had been there a long time. This revelation piqued my curiosity and generated many questions: When did they come? Where did they come from? How did they get there? I asked her if she knew the history of her mother's family in Nova Scotia, and she knew names, but not their origin. She also knew they came to the Windsor area a few generations ago.

In 2016, I began to delve into my own Scottish genealogy and met a Canadian woman from British Columbia, the furthest western province of the country. She and her husband were Scottish also, and she was more than happy to help me with my Scottish search.

I inquired about her knowledge of black Canadians in Nova Scotia. She said she had never met a black Canadian in her part of the country but would do a little research. She emailed me the name of a group of people I had no knowledge of: Black Loyalists.

The History of the Black Loyalists

The origin of the name Black Loyalist dates back to the end of the American Revolution. The British Loyalists, upon defeat by colonial Patriots, signed the 1783 Treaty of Paris, which, in part, set the terms for the British withdrawal from the country with their employees and property.

Southern slave owners, classifying slaves as property, wanted the British to return those slaves who had escaped their plantations and gone behind enemy lines to fight for the British, upon a promise of freedom. The British, wanting to keep their promise to those who had fought for them, insisted they take the former slaves with them. At a minimum, the slave owners wanted to be compensated for this loss. A Book of Negroes was created, documenting numbers and listing names of those blacks for whom compensation would be paid.

By 1783, the British government issued land grants in Nova Scotia for the defeated population of loyalists. Blacks either employed by the British in northern states or who fought for them during the war were put on a ship headed to this Canadian province. Here they would start a new life.

Between 1776 and 1783, approximately 3,000 Black Loyalists, along with the British Loyalists, arrived in Nova Scotia by ship, docking in the southeast area then known as Port Roseway, now Shelburne County. They formed the small rural community of Birchtown, adjacent to the white community of Birch. Could Sheila's maternal ancestors, the Taylors, have been in this group?

Another Water Crossing

In the early to mid-1700s, Amherstburg was a British military post in Detroit, named after the British army officer who defeated the French at Detroit. At the time of the Treaty of Paris in 1783, when British loyalists were withdrawing from the United States after their loss in the American Revolutionary War, the British government awarded land grants to those citizens to move not only to Nova Scotia, but other areas, such as Upper Canada (now Ontario), to settle and farm in small communities in the areas of Amherstburg, Colchester, and Harrow, in the farthest southwestern parts of Canada.

In total, 50,000 British loyalists sought refuge in all Canadian provinces, mostly Quebec, Nova Scotia, and the Maritime Provinces. But in 1790, 20,000 people called the "late loyalists" settled in Upper Canada, the current province of Ontario.

Over the next seventy years, over 30,000 slaves and freedmen seeking refugee crossed the Detroit River, known by the code word "Midnight." They entered Canada at what is now Windsor under the cover of darkness, by row and other flat-bottomed boats, hidden under docks at Detroit's waterfront. Later, they would come by steamship to Amherstburg, where the river meets Lake Erie. There, the abolitionist ship's steward and captain would unload their "lumber."

The new arrivals raised crops, felled timber, started newspapers, built churches and schools, and learned to read and write. But their presence in the community was not welcomed by all. Irish and German immigrants, former loyalists, often from the South, were trying to make a living in the area as well. They brought their prejudices with them, particularly as the number of blacks grew, and they prospered harvesting lumber.

Then came the Civil War. Thousands of black Canadians joined the Union Army through a recruitment center at the Second Baptist Church on Monroe Street in Detroit. Many were heavily recruited by the abolitionists in the United States.

While Canada took a neutral stance during the war, the fugitives knew that their own future, as well as the future of their relatives living in the United States, was dependent on the outcome of the war. And although they would originally form a "Colored Corp" because of segregation in the military, they joined without reservation.

The Union prevailed, and the refugees now were free from the reach of southern slaveholders in the United States. Because most saw the land in the United States as their birthright, and because of the strong family connections many Canadian blacks still had in the United States, this was their 'home.' Within several years after the war ended, two-thirds of the 30,000 blacks living in Canada recrossed the border back into the United States to live.

Sheila Kersey Harris's paternal great-grandfather was not one of them, and several descendant families of those early freedom-seekers were still residents of Amherstburg and the southern communities of Colchester and Harrow at the time of Sheila's childhood. She remembers the Harrises, the Wilsons, the Handsers, the Hursts, the Stuarts, Maxine Banks, and four McCurdy families.

SHEILA KERSEY HARRIS:
INTERNATIONAL BORDER CROSSING—
FOR BETTER OR FOR WORSE

The Birds Are Sad Today

It's a bright Saturday morning in November of 2017 on Lodewyck Street on Detroit's eastside. A 5'3" black woman stands in the small front yard of her redbrick bungalow, holding a plastic bag full of breadcrumbs. It is 10:00 a.m., and this is the second time she has been in this space to feed the wrens and house sparrows—at least thirty of them.

"This is the bread that is going stale. These birds might as well have it. I feed the squirrels too."

Sheila Harris, with a complexion the color of milk coffee and white/grey wavy hair, has engaged in this routine of feeding the birds for most of the twenty years she and her husband Michael have lived on this street. The birds display an uncanny comfort level with her.

"When the birds see me open the front door and walk down the three steps, they fly in and wait for me to get to the sidewalk with their bread. They are not skittish and do not fly off when I'm there. When Michael feeds them instead, they wait until he has left before they fly in."

But in one month, the birds will no longer have their benefactor. Sheila and Michael are moving away. The extended family on both sides of this family unit is in the Detroit-Windsor, Ontario area, and all their previous moves have been within the region. They are walking away from the only place they have ever known—a place that has brought them unspeakable sorrow, but joy too.

Childhood Homes in Amherstburg and Windsor, Canada

Sheila Beatrice Kersey was a postwar baby, born in Windsor, Ontario,

Canada, on November 6, 1946, the second oldest daughter and one of seven children, six of whom survived past their first year. She spent her childhood in homes in either Windsor or Amherstburg, eighteen miles apart on the Ojibway Parkway, and in one of the original black settlements in a region at the mouth of the Detroit River where it intersects Lake Erie.

Her parents, Elmer and Effie, worked different shifts. Windsor is the auto capital of Canada, and Elmer worked afternoons at Walker Metals, a subsidy of Chrysler, where they made engine casts. He rose from assembly to become a foreman. Her mother was a nurse's aide, working the day shift at a Windsor hospital.

Sheila would become responsible for caretaking. Floretta, the oldest daughter, had type 1 diabetes, and Sheila remembers, as a small girl, administering Floretta's shot of insulin in her leg. She also had primary responsibility for taking care of her younger brother Bobbie first, and then four others to follow.

First Recognition of Racial Divisions

When Sheila was in first and second grade, she, her brother, and older sister were the only blacks who attended Catholic school in Windsor, when her family moved there to care for her paternal grandfather. She doesn't recall any problems between blacks and whites.

"There were black families ahead of us in school. We were in a very mixed neighborhood, with mostly French and Italian residents. My aunt married a Frenchman. Everyone knew one another, but the only black families in the neighborhood were named Bayliss, Riley, Crosby, Scott, Gross, Johnson, and Taylor."

After her grandfather's death, they moved back to Amherstburg, where the family remained until Sheila was in seventh grade. Here began her first recognition of racial discrimination because they were not allowed to go to the Catholic school there.

"I couldn't figure out why we didn't go to the Catholic school in Amherstburg. I had my first communion in Windsor and then prepared for confirmation. While we attended church there, we didn't go to school there.

"Actually, my mother felt we would be safer in the public school. After school, there were fights between the white kids from the Catholic school and the black kids from the public school. They actually had to stagger the times the kids got out to avoid confrontations. The Catholic schoolkids got out a half hour early.

"Sometimes, the Protestants and Catholics fought, too."

But racial tensions were never far away. Sheila remembers a time when her brothers were accused of theft.

"They rode their new bikes down the street to play with kids who were new on the block.

"After the boys came home, the white man from that house came to our house and accused the boys of taking his son's trucks and cars. My dad asked me if the boys had brought these toys home. I said, 'No, they were on their bikes.'"

Sheila's dad was outraged that the man would not inquire first, but accused his sons outright.

"I was so afraid my father would fight with the man. It turned out someone else had taken the toys. Even after this fact became known, he wouldn't apologize. My father went to the man and said, 'You called my daughter and sons liars. You need to apologize.'"

The man eventually was forced to apologize—Sheila was still reluctant to accept his apology. But her father made her.

"The man finally said that he knew my parents were bringing us up right."

Daddy's Girl and Sports

"I was really close to my dad. My mother was working every day, and I had to take care of the four younger kids."

On weekends, Sheila remembers going with her dad and her younger brothers to play baseball, and hockey, and to skate. She appeared to be a budding Olympian in women's hockey. But, she had to trick her little brother, Bobbie, first.

"When the skates were handed out, I got the figure skates and Bobbie got the hockey skates. I wanted to play hockey. The figure skates didn't interest me. So I switched skates with Bobbie. He was pretty young, and he didn't know any better. I used his skates to play hockey and gave him my figure skates. I eventually got my own pair of hockey skates and played for a number of years."

In spite of racial tensions between some kids at public and private schools, Sheila only remembers an integrated neighborhood as she was growing up. The small percentage of blacks in the area, less than four percent out of a total Windsor population of approximately 114,000 (1960 census), were disbursed throughout the Windsor area.

"Even in Amherstburg, from day one, I didn't know there were any differences in people. Sure, I saw the color differences, but, we kids still called the French white people aunts and uncles. Plus, there were interracial marriages in my family. Some of my aunts and uncles lived in Detroit."

The international border between Windsor and Detroit was a border in name only for the Kersey family. Several of Sheila's maternal aunts and uncles lived in Detroit, and the only international tunnel in the world provided the route to visit them.

"We used to come across on the bus through the tunnel all the time. When you were little, you could come across free. Then, we had to use tokens. So my mother would buy ten for a dollar. We would go shopping at Hudson's and Woolworth's at Christmastime and visit relatives.

"Two of my aunts, Arita and Madeline, lived in Detroit, and we had lots of cousins there."

Graduation, Jobs, and Marriage

Sheila graduated from high school in Windsor in 1964. Following in her mother's footsteps, she tried to work as a nurse's aide at Riverview Hospital on Riverside Drive in Windsor, but she couldn't handle it. "It was mainly older and disabled people, and I wasn't prepared for that."

She went to the unemployment office to apply for work. There were welding jobs available at Fabco, which fabricated steel. A man came to the house and began to ask her father whether his sons might want to going into welding.

"Do they take women," Sheila asked.

"We do take women." But the man looked skeptical.

"I think she'd be well suited, as she has worked on cars with me," said Sheila's father.

Sheila went for training, received her welding license, and started a job doing MIG and metal arc welding in wheels. Then, she met Henry Rogers. She was introduced to him by a mutual friend at a party in Windsor. He was black and from Milwaukee. She was still eighteen years old when they married.

Her relationship with her in-laws did not start out well. She didn't meet his family until after the wedding.

"I met Henry's mother on our honeymoon in Milwaukee after we got married. His mother wanted to know why I didn't invite them to the wedding. I told her I had asked Henry to invite them. But, he didn't. She always held this against me. Plus, here I was a light-skinned Canadian coming and 'taking' an American black man.

"Our cultures were different. I didn't act like the women in his family.

I didn't talk slang, and I was into sports. We had nothing in common, so I didn't have anything to talk to them about."

Three children would be born of the marriage: Brian Jeffrey in 1969, Genee in 1970, and Rochelle in 1972. While the marriage would not last, Sheila maintained a strong bond with her father.

"My dad had bought a baby outfit a few days before Rochelle was born. He said he knew the baby was a girl. We had gone to a funeral of a friend's daughter. My dad said, 'You will be doing this to me (burying me) soon.' Within two weeks he was dead. He hadn't been sick, but he died of a massive heart attack. I was devastated."

Middle Years: Children and Seniors

As the kids grew, Sheila worked jobs around her children's and Henry's schedule. In the early 1980s, she worked as an aide at the Brian Hislop Home in Windsor, a home for children removed from their own homes because of abuse or neglect. She worked the overnight shift, and her main duty was to ensure that the children did not leave the building. Every night, her children called to tell her good night before they went to bed.

The children got older, and she and Henry became more estranged. Her son Brian began attending college in Windsor, Genee graduated and began retail work in Windsor, and Rochelle was finishing high school. The children were living at home with their father in Windsor, and Sheila began to look for a second job in Detroit.

She wasn't afraid of hard physical work, and began doing residential cleaning and painting for apartment complexes in the city. She met a painter who was married to Virginia Harris, the sister of Michael Harris and five other siblings. Sheila began to spend time with the Harris family, and in particular Michael, in Detroit, and her children met and spent time with many of the Harris children. At the time, Michael was a Detroit police officer.

The owner of several apartment complexes took notice of Sheila's strong work ethic. She began taking on additional duties for them, including collecting rent checks in buildings where there was no resident manager. They remained impressed, noting that she could handle herself well. Would she consider moving into the Colony Arms Senior Apartments on Jefferson Avenue, a main east-west thoroughfare in Detroit, a few miles from the tunnel, and becoming the resident manager during the day? The timing was right.

"I moved into one of the two joined buildings. The first thing I noticed was that sometimes the residents had a tough time getting to the grocery store. I wanted to make sure they had access to fresh food. So I had a guy come and set up a little farmer's market, selling fresh vegetables and fruits at the buildings. Then, there was a milkman who sold milk and butter there. We had barbeque picnics in the back lot. Residents seemed to appreciate all of these little things."

Not all people in the neighborhood appreciated Sheila, however—she was a one-woman patrol when it came to the prostitutes.

"They knew I didn't want them in the apartments and would scatter when they saw me coming out of the buildings. They knew when the men got their Social Security checks, and they would follow them to the little corner store to get their checks cashed and come back to their apartment. I knew there wasn't much I could do. But, one time, I had to take control.

"Her name was Janice, and she was a regular. She was with a man in his apartment, and she wanted more money from him. The janitor came to me because he heard the man screaming for help.

"I took the master key and went over to his apartment. Janice was beating him with the broom. She wasn't dressed. I said, 'Get dressed and leave.' She said, 'I'm not leaving.' I had the janitor take the screen out of the window and told her she was either going to go down the steps or she was going out the window. The apartment was on a low level, and I helped her leave through the window."

Sheila tried to stay healthy herself, walking seven mornings a week—5:00 a.m. to be exact. She would meet several other women at downtown apartment complexes, and as a group of six, they would walk around a city block—four miles each weekday. One dark morning, the women saw a man removing a hubcap from the wheel of a car. The women stopped, paralyzed by the thought that they might be victimized.

"Don't worry guys, I have a hand gun," Sheila said, shocking her friends when she pulled it out of her pocket. She had a permit to carry a concealed weapon because she carried large sums of money for her job, and it stayed in her pocket at all times. This was the only time they witnessed criminal activity.

The Last Border Crossing

At the time Sheila started working days in Detroit, she continued working the midnight shift at the Brian Hislop home in Windsor. As she was crossing through the Detroit-Windsor tunnel daily, her daughter Genee, now twenty-one, was also making friends in Detroit. She would regularly visit her mother at the Colony Arms.

In January of 1991, Genee disappeared. She had received a call in the middle of the night in Windsor, called a cab, and had the cabdriver drop her off on a street corner on Detroit's eastside. Her sister Rochelle didn't think much about Genee leaving the house then, but, by the next morning when she wasn't home, she called her mom.

Sheila knew that Genee had friends, maybe a boyfriend, on the east side of Detroit, so she began to canvass the area, contacted the police, and the boyfriend. He claimed to know nothing. She had flyers made listing an 800 number to call and posted them on telephone posts and in stores. She worked with police on names of possible friends to be interviewed.

"I got all of the addresses for the police. I talked to a number of police sergeants over time at that eastside precinct. I kept a list of who I talked to and the date."

This went on for months. "Every time television news indicated a body was found somewhere in the metropolitan area, I called."

Then, in June, the Windsor police received a call that a decomposed body had been found by two fishermen in the water at the mouth of the Detroit River. They didn't know what it was because it was tied up in a tarp. The police contacted the Wayne County Sheriff's Department on the Detroit side of the river to check their records for missing persons.

The body wore a shirt that had a Canadian Maple leaf on it. A deputy remembered talking to Sheila about the fact that her daughter was a Canadian resident. Dental records were needed to confirm identity.

"I remember going to the Wayne County morgue with Michael. He went inside to talk to the workers. At the time, he had been a police officer for twenty years and knew the ropes.

"He came out into the lobby and said they didn't want me to see the body. I was okay with that. I always knew she was gone, but, when they finally found the body, it was almost a relief. *I got my child back.*

"My mission to find my daughter had come to an end. I had been hurting so bad. And to have her back and not to have to worry about where she was and if someone was hurting her was a blessing. I had so many nightmares, so many nights when I didn't sleep." *She's with me always now.*"

The Aftermath

The family was devastated. Genee's sister, Rochelle, at first wouldn't get out of bed for days. Her brother, Jeffrey, went into a rage, drinking and fighting, blaming Americans for the death of his sister. Sheila told him, "Jeffrey, you can't say that. Your father is an American from Milwaukee." Then, Jeffrery had a car accident, and she was able to get him and his sister into group counseling.

"I started going to counseling because I started having hallucinations. A guy at work said, 'Sheila I think you need help dealing with your daughter's death.'

"I went to counseling, and I took a class in Windsor for Parents of Murdered Children. I was in a group, and at the end of one and a half years, they wanted me to lead the group. I did that for a while.

"Henry finally had a nervous breakdown. He had been in denial the whole time Genee was gone, saying, 'She'll be home.' The ambulance came for Henry when Jeffrey was home. He called me in Detroit, and I went to the hospital in Windsor. The doctor asked me if I knew what was going on with him. I told him that Henry had a lot going on with his daughter's death. The doctor said he remembered reading about the girl's death in the newspaper, but he didn't connect the name, and Henry didn't tell him. Henry recovered, but continued to have heart problems that led to his death when he was in his sixties.

Genee's memorial service was at the Windsor Chapel on Tecumseh Road on June 29, 1991. But the cloud of death would hover still. Sheila's then-boyfriend Michael Harris's son, Keven Dyer Harris, one year older than Genee, would be killed in a drive-by shooting coming out of his home on Detroit's west side on August 12, 1991.

Forty-five days after Genee's memorial service, Sheila would be sitting in the front row of one of the viewing rooms at the James H.

Cole Funeral Home on Grand River in Detroit for Kevin's funeral. Both murders remain unsolved.

The Copper Canyon: A Neighborhood Dies

Michigan Public Act 212 of 1999, entitled the Residency of Public Employees Act, prohibits municipalities from requiring city employees to live in the city where they work. This statute had received heavy support from the Detroit Police Officers Association, which desperately wanted its membership to have the right to live wherever they chose. They won.

Prior to the law's effective date, white Detroit police officers and firefighters lived on several blocks on either Detroit's east side or west side in mostly redbrick bungalows, which backed up to the city's border. Those neighborhoods became known as "Copper Canyon." Once the statute took effect, white officers moved en masse to suburbs in another county.

The former Detroit neighborhoods, predictably, became areas of rental homes. While Sheila and Michael, after their marriage in 1995, were able to purchase a well-kept bungalow for themselves, they had a constant influx of new people in their neighborhood. And, over the years, more and more young people moved in who had no problem keeping the neighbors up at night with their loud music.

A One-Woman Neighborhood Watch

Sheila and Michael continued to keep the appearance of their home up as the area continued to change. They were the first to shovel their sidewalks when it snowed and mow their lawn in the spring and summer. Sheila put up Christmas lights and had lawn decorations for Halloween. The kids in the neighborhood came to her house first for Halloween candy.

The city set up neighborhood community programs to try to preserve the area and targeted Sheila to become a block captain. She proved to be the right person—she was fearless.

"I would knock on doors and tell people about keeping up their property when they moved in. I would get them to bring in their garbage containers. Every time something would happen, like a fire or a fight, I usually was the one who called the police."

But sometimes there were evictions, and then vacant houses. One such house, another redbrick bungalow on the corner, was right across the street from the Harris house. Squatters moved into it during the summer.

"Then, when the weather was getting cold, they began stealing electricity from DTE (Detroit Electric) from the house next door that was also vacant. I called DTE, and they came and cut the line between the two houses.

"One morning Michael was going to work at 5:00 a.m., and he said the house across the street was on fire; flames were shooting through the roof and out of the back of the house.

The roof collapsed, and I kept calling for the city to demolish the house. I called the city often, talking to many different people. I kept calling them, and finally after six months, the house came down. By that time, they knew me by my first name."

"But I wasn't done. They left a big hole in the ground, another unsafe condition. I kept calling them again, a different department. This time it only took a few months for them to fill the hole. It's now just an empty lot on the corner with overgrown weeds."

One More Challenge

As if the stresses of losing a daughter and Michael's son in the most violent way, and living in a declining neighborhood, were not challenging enough, there would be another serious stressor. In the last months of

2014, Sheila was diagnosed with breast cancer. On February 10, 2015, she had a left-breast mastectomy, and in August 2016, she had reconstruction surgery. The cancer is gone for now.

For a while, Sheila was down for the count. But many neighbors rallied around their block captain, bringing in food and doing chores. Her neighbors on both sides mowed her lawn. Some took her to her doctor's appointments because Michael was still working. Sheila was surprised and grateful for the care and concern of her neighbors.

On a December day in 2017, the week before Christmas, Sheila prepared her last Christmas dinner for the extended Rogers-Harris clan that now included four generations. Yet again, she managed to pack close to twenty people into the basement, placing card tables and chairs in every conceivable spot.

Within days, Sheila and Michael would be packing up a U-Haul and moving to North Fort Myers, Florida, where they will live a few hours from her daughter and a few hours from her brother Bobbie, from whom she commandeered that pair of hockey skates many decades ago.

She was leaving behind snow shoveling, lawn mowing, and responsibility for trying to preserve a neighborhood and losing the battle. Six decades of taking care of others would now be behind her, and she could concentrate on her own care—her biggest decision these days being whether to walk or take the golf cart to water aerobics.

PART II

GROWING ROOTS

— 4 —

ALICE BARLASS

Photo Credit: Author

MEETING ALICE

After many years of living in the rural Midwest, I have drawn some conclusions about children raised on the farm. They may be broad generalities, but for me they ring true.

I have heard that a farmer's first love is land—now I believe it. A farm has a sense of place different from anywhere else. A person who grows up on a farm that raised or used animals, is close to nature and the rhythms of life and death; they know the loss of an animal is a part of farm life. By the age of eighteen, they have seen more animals die than most have in a lifetime. Nonetheless, farm life gets in their blood. They have fed animals on Christmas morning (some animals even get presents), in pouring rain, sweltering heat. It is hard work, but they can't imagine doing anything else.

Some young people raised on a farm don't feel this way, of course; they run like mad to get away from the farm when they come of age. My mother did this back in 1935. She left a South Dakota farm to come to Detroit, and never looked back. Perhaps this is the reason I know so little about caring for the land and animals and am now so curious about life on the land.

But for many adults, the pull of the land is magnetic. Perhaps, it has something to do with a love and respect for nature. Jerry Apps, Wisconsin author of *Whispers and Shadows: A Naturalist's Memoir*, who grew up on a farm, says when you grow up on a farm, you learn to live with nature and not struggle against it. "Nature will dictate your life. It lets you know that you are not in charge. We had a certain reverence for nature."

When living in two Moo Towns, one in Rock County, Wisconsin, the other in Eaton County, Michigan, I met women who either grew up on the farm and left or are still living on a farm and working the land.

Most of the women in this second group were over forty-five years of age. Although they took jobs off the farm for family income, they still had a strong connection to the land. They had livestock or crops, sometimes both, and the remainder of their day after their regular job consisted of working the land and/or feeding the animals.

If they had crops, their activities were dictated by the planting and harvesting seasons. If an old barn sat on the property, there were barn cats. If they cultivated fruit trees, there was canned bounty. Their gardens may have been small, but they regularly used their produce to prepare meals.

Even though they left the farm of their youth, they found a way to come back to live on the land. This is where they are spending their adult years—this is where they will die. Alice Barlass is one of these women. But her story has deeper historical roots than most. Her husband's family, the Barlasses, were one of four founding farm families in the Rock Valley Prairie in the mid-1800s, and the local historical archives are replete with Barlass family history.

HISTORICAL CONTEXT

The Coming of the Scots to Wisconsin

A 170-year-old black steamer trunk sits on the sturdy oak floor in the second-story hallway of a homestead on County Road A in Janesville, Wisconsin, the only remaining symbol of the Barlass family trans-Atlantic journey to the Milwaukee area in the mid-1840s.

Several factors influenced the immigration of Scottish peoples during this time. Strict inheritance laws favoring large landowners had denied some Scots their own land. Further, Scotland had never had enough resources, minerals, or land to provide a living for all of the male children born there.

In the 1830s came news that farming country in America's fertile prairie was being formed into states from the Northwest Territory. Upon learning land there was going for $1.25 per acre, many rushed to leave Glasgow. Men bid farewell to their families and crossed the Atlantic to New York, a six-week endeavor. From there the trip to the prospective farmland continued through the Erie Canal and the Great Lakes to Chicago and Milwaukee.

But when the Scots arrived in Milwaukee, they spoke a different language than the prominent German immigrant population already in place, making communication a struggle. Some became discouraged and made plans to return to Scotland.

On one such day when four Scottish families went to the land office to purchase their steamer tickets to return to Scotland, they met another Scot who had gone there to sell his produce—Andrew Barlass. He told them not to leave but rather to come with him to a place not far away— Emerald Grove—where they could homestead.

The Immigrant Story of Andrew Barlass

Pioneer Andrew Barlass, born in the parish of Kinross, Scotland, on September 30, 1822, crossed the Atlantic on a sailing vessel from Glasgow to New York in 1842 at the age of nineteen. He was looking for a better life for himself, his mother Mary, and his siblings. His father, David, had died in his twenties in a farming accident, leaving the family with no means of support.

Andrew made his way by a lake steamer to Chicago, where he secured a team of horses and continued his travels on an old plank road to south-central Wisconsin. His uncle was already a farmer in the region, giving Andrew the ability to farm for him for two years until he could purchase eighty acres of land for himself.

In 1844, his mother Mary and younger brother David arrived in the Rock Prairie Valley, then known as the paradise of the West. Over the years, Andrew purchased more than 200 acres, leaving forty acres for timberland and utilizing the rest for his home farm. Here he raised and sold Clydesdale horses and Durham cattle, acquiring great wealth.

There was more to Andrew's life than farming. He loved music and was said to be present at every Scottish gathering in the region, particularly at the Burns Festival (named after poet Robert Burns). He sang old Scottish ballads and played the violin so that the lads and lasses could dance the old-fashioned Scottish reel. For many years, he led church hymns.

In his middle years, this stern-looking, tall, slender, bearded man was called to public life. He served in many local and state offices, beginning with assessor and justice of the peace, then proceeding to town and county supervisor. But his greatest achievement was being elected to the Wisconsin General Assembly from Rock County for two terms, with nary a challenger.

When Andrew was in his sixties, he met with misfortune on his farm (eerily reminiscent of his father); he was killed from a kick by one of his mares. His July 27, 1895 obituary indicates that the kick came with such force that it shattered three of his ribs into fragments, resulting in extensive internal bleeding.

But his end was not *the* end. Today, 120 years later, because of Alice Barlass, the next three generations continue Andrew's legacy.

ALICE BARLASS:
WEDDED TO LAND AND LIVESTOCK

"If we have no history, we have no future." —Alice

Intro to Farm Life

She stands on the stoop of the 116-year-old white-frame house on Highway A, waiting for the visitor's car to pull into the circular, dirt driveway. Flowerbeds adorn the small porch on both sides. It is the end of April, and daffodils and irises bloom with more of their green shoots peeking through the ground. She has lived in this double-peaked grey house with white trim and a second-floor balcony with spindled railings for over thirty-five years. While her husband's family staked a claim to this property in the early 1900s, it is she who now calls this home.

Alice Tolberson Barlass, a grandmotherly figure with white, wavy hair, glasses, and a warm smile, grew up on a Holstein dairy farm in southeast Wisconsin not far from her current home and has been raising livestock and crops with her family ever since. She recently celebrated her eighty-seventh birthday. If she has anything to say about it—even though she is not planning on going anywhere and has all her paperwork in order—she will die at home, much like her mother. Until the day she died, her mother walked fifty feet out to the mailbox and back twice a day every day of the week for exercise.

Her life story began fifteen miles northeast of Whitewater, but when she was eight, her family moved to a home two and one half miles from her current residence. The only time she lived anywhere else was when she attended a local university, and even then, she came home on weekends. She originally thought she might follow in her sister's foot-steps and attend the University of Wisconsin-Madison, but she found that college too overwhelming.

Alice finds tremendous comfort in staying in place—a homebody—in the best sense of the word. Even today, when her son offers to take her on a short trip to see her sister in Ohio, she prefers to stay put and use the telephone instead. She has always been that way.

Growing Up with Animals

Farm animals always have been in Alice's life—starting with her first chore of feeding her family's laying hens. They would forage in the shade of the oak trees all day, a feeder placed close to two milk cans full of water.

"Around 5:00 or 6:00 p.m. my dad and I would try to corral 300 chickens to go into the henhouse to save them from being eaten by a mink during the night."

Ensuring the safety of the chickens was paramount, so Alice's father had built them an elaborate house.

"It was quite nice, actually: two insulated rooms with straw boxes on the shelves. It was a cozy place with southern exposure windows. The range shelter was an enclosed small house with chicken wire all around it. It had moveable planks." Water was kept clear in the winter with a small, low-grade oil fountain heating it.

Eggs were a significant source of family income in addition to milk produced by Holstein cows. Alice's connection to the eggs and farm remained strong even while she lived in a resident hall at the University of Wisconsin-Whitewater. She would come home every weekend to help clean and sort the eggs.

"We had a Chicago business. People came up on a Monday afternoon to get ninety dozen eggs. Those eggs had to be white. If they weren't white, we had to wash them carefully at the outside spigot. But the goal was to keep them clean from the time of collection to the time of sale."

Teaching and Marriage

A 1952 University of Wisconsin graduate, with an education major, Alice was teaching in a local school district when she met Marvin Barlass. He was a fourth-generation farmer in a distinguished Scottish family that in 1844 arrived in Rock County. Continuing his family's agricultural tradition, he began to farm the area and eventually raise Jersey cows.

After they married, Alice helped on the farm in addition to teaching. Seven days a week she would rise at 4:30 a.m. and go to the barn to set up the vacuum-pump milk lines that would begin the process for milking the Jersey cows. Some were milked three times a day, others two.

Their family was growing (eventually three boys and two girls) when she was considered for a principal position. Since they had enough financial stability through their dairy farm and crops, they decided she should stay home and raise the children.

Alice continued to make a contribution to farm operations by preparing lunch for the workers. Particularly for the fifteen-hour days during planting and harvesting seasons, she made sandwiches so the workers would not lose time away from the fields. She still does.

Marvin died in 2008, but by then the Barlass sons had learned all the farm operations. Five hundred acres were under the plow; they planted corn, soybeans, rye, and winter wheat. But most importantly, there were over four hundred Jersey cows to milk—now using machines and two shifts of workers. For many decades, the Barlass name and Jersey cows have been spoken in one breath.

Barlass History and Jersey Cows

Over one hundred years ago, the Barlass family of Rock County, Wisconsin, began raising Jersey cows. Today, Alice Barlass and the next two generations are raising Jersey cows not only in Wisconsin, but also in

California. Her grandson, Brett, has an operation of five thousand Jerseys, a breed that is second highest in number in the world after Holsteins.

The Barlasses do more than raise cows; their contributions to the dairy industry and the Jersey cattle breed, in particular, are legendary. In fact, in 2016, Alice, as the head of the Barlass clan, was publicly recognized for her contribution to the breed at the annual American Jersey Cattle Association (AJCA) meeting in San Diego.

Two generations of Barlasses are active at a national level in the American Jersey Cattle Association, with Alice's daughter Sara being a regional representative over six northeastern states. She travels throughout the United States "scoring" the cows when the quality of a Jersey herd needs to be appraised. Recently, she was sent to California to score cows close to the forest fires. Granddaughter Kristen also works for the Jersey Cattle Association.

Over 200,000 Jersey cows are registered in the world. They have an illustrious history, are unique in their features with their fawn color and black nose with a white band around it, and produce milk with more protein and fat content than other dairy cows. Females are known to have a gentler disposition than other breeds.

While the origin of the Jerseys cannot be determined, it is believed that they were brought to Jersey Island, the largest of the Channel Islands in the English Channel off the coast of France, hundreds of years ago by the French. Because the government wanted to keep the breed pure, in 1763, legislation was passed to prevent the importation of other cattle to the island. Eighty years later, the British Agricultural and Horticultural Society began exporting cattle to the United States. In 1866, the Herd Book began, tracking the lineage of each cow so that future buyers could authenticate its purity.

The cows are now sold worldwide, with the highest prices for those with the highest percentage of milk fat and protein. The milk is used extensively in the production of yogurt. Jerseys continue to be a significant force in agriculture production on the Island, but their future there was not always assured.

The Jersey breed was in jeopardy during World War II. The Isle of Jersey, as well as its sister Isle of Guernsey (British Crown dependencies called Bailiwicks), were the only British possessions occupied by the Germans beginning in 1940, when up to 100,000 troops were stationed on the islands.

One person is credited with saving some of the best Jerseys during that time—fourteen-year-old Anne Elizabeth Billot. So strong was Anne's loyalty to the Jerseys, that she and a few other girlfriends hid some of the best in a cave in the forest so that they would not be slaughtered for their meat to feed the German troops in Poland. Once a day, they would go into the dark caves to feed the cows, not even allowing themselves a flashlight, for fear of being caught by the Germans.

After the war, Anne was hailed as a hero and became involved in the World Jersey Cattle Bureau and the Lord Jersey Research Trust, a research and development arm of the bureau. In 1978, upon a visit by Queen Elizabeth to the isle, one of her Jerseys was selected out of more than a thousand candidates as a gift to the queen. Forty years later, the affection of the queen for Jerseys was mentioned in a program leading up to the wedding of the Duke and Duchess of Sussex.

In 2011, Anne Billot Preschard came to Wisconsin as an honoree at the World Jersey Dairy Conference held at the World Dairy Expo annual convention in Madison. She stayed in the home of Alice Barlass, where she told the family her story of the Jersey cows during the war. Alice recorded the details for posterity. Upon the occasion of Anne's death in 2013 at the age of eighty-one, a film honoring her commitment to the improvement and promotion of the Jersey breed was produced. It is housed at the research facility on the Isle of Jersey.

Alice's Life Today

Alice is deeply religious and regularly attends services at the Rock Prairie United Presbyterian Church, a successor to the Reformed Presbyterian Church of Rock Prairie the Barlass family helped charter in 1847. She has been active in Farm Wives, previously having been given the award of Jersey Wife of the Year at the Wisconsin Dairy Expo.

In her ninth decade, she remains active in Zonta, an international service organization that advances the status of women, and attends the monthly lunches of the University of Wisconsin-Whitewater Alumni Association, although she sees fewer of her 1952 classmates every year.

She still sends Christmas cards. Recently, she had an idea to make her own photo card by using one of her Jersey calves. She went to the barn with her camera and a Santa Claus hat, but every time she reached to place the hat on the calf's head, it backed away before she could take a photo. Finally, in frustration, she gave up, came back into the house, and gave her Christmas card order for a Jersey cow card to her son to be included with his order. She sends a Jersey cow card every year.

When Alice reflects on her home's legacy, she thinks of Helen Barlass, her husband's aunt, who never married. "She lived here by herself for fifty years, but she prepared Sunday dinner for the entire family every week." She chuckles when she recalls one memorable Sunday, when, Helen, apparently not realizing she spilled flour on the floor, traipsed it all over the dining room, big white footprints following her everywhere. "Maybe her eyesight was getting bad," Alice quipped.

When Helen died, she was buried in the Johnston Township Cemetery. Alice names all the Barlasses who are buried in that cemetery—Andrew, Christina, Isabel, Marion, Helen, and Catherine Barlass from

Florida—many generations. "It seems to be the old folks place. Such a comforting place for our family."

She is at peace with the fact that she will join the other Barlasses in this, her final resting place, in the not-too-distant future.

— 5 —

GLADYS "RUSTY" DELAND

Gladys "Rusty" Deland　　　　　*Sharon Deland*

Photo Credit: Rod Weaver

MEETING GLADYS

Seeing women in their eighties and nineties exercising at the fitness center brings joy to my heart. Their bodies are healthy, they have active minds, and they make time to spend with friends. Others don't seem to notice them, but I am drawn to these strong women. This is how I want to be at that age; this is how I wish my mother had lived her life. But she never made it to her eighties—nor her seventies.

I met Gladys in 2014. "She has bright red hair. You can't miss her," my friend said. "She's in her mid-nineties." He thought she would be a good subject of interest for one of my articles in the local community newspaper, *The County Journal*. Sure enough, I knew exactly whom he meant; she was hard to miss.

Gladys Deland was a member of MOVE, the fitness club sponsored by Hayes Green Beach Hospital in Charlotte (pop. 9,200) in south central Michigan. This is where she arrived three mornings a week, entering through the sliding glass doors with her red walker. My enchantment with Gladys was immediate. She was not only in her mid-nineties, and she had hair the color of rust.

"Everyone calls me Rusty," she said in a deep, raspy voice. "I always hated the name Gladys." She decided to change her name (unofficially) when she worked at the bowling alley. "I didn't like Gladys, or Red or Happy Bottom—names they called me at the bowling alley. There was a lady on the radio at the time called Rusty Warren, so I told everyone from here on out to call me Rusty." It worked.

After meeting Gladys, I was eager to learn about her life's journey and how it might have contributed to her being strong enough to leg press 125 pounds (the same weight I pressed when starting at the fitness center).

Gladys is the oldest person who comes to the fitness center. How is it that a woman in her tenth decade climbs onto the treadmill and pushes the start button, slowly increasing the speed? True enough, she has an aide standing by, but still, what motivates her? When Gladys was born, a treadmill was not even on the horizon as an exercise machine.

She arrives at the fitness center with her seventy-one-year-old daughter, Sharon, who drives them in a white 4 x 4 pickup truck with a stenciled black horse on the left rear panel. Sharon wears glasses, has flawless skin, penetrating blue eyes, and short, gunmetal grey hair. But the thing that caught my eye first is that she walks with crutches because she only has one good leg. The other is amputated above the knee.

The two women use different machines—Sharon uses only upper body and abdominal machines, Gladys uses the treadmill and does leg presses to develop stronger leg muscles, so she won't fall again.

GLADYS DELAND:
HARDSHIP & SIMPLE LIVING IN RURAL MIDWEST

Gladys's Early Years

"If this story is about my life, there is not a bit of it I'd like to live over—my childhood was not what I would have wanted," she says. But live on she would, well past all of her friends, now approaching her ninety-eighth birthday.

In July of 1919, Gladys McMannis was the firstborn of four in the small rural village of Richland, one square mile in size, in south central Michigan. The next in line, Lucille, was born with muscular dystrophy, and her disability ended Gladys's childhood freedom. Lucille could only walk with great difficulty, and Gladys had to take her everywhere. She had to be included in all the things Gladys wanted to do, "dragging her in the wagon," wherever she went. She never left the house without Lucille.

But as if Lucille's constant presence wasn't bad enough, she had an attitude—a bad one.

"My sister was hateful."

The older she got, the more resentful she became, and life became unbearable for Gladys.

"Not only did I have to take her to school, I had to take her to Sunday school."

Since Lucille couldn't use the wagon here, she "crawled on her hands and knees up the front steps of the Church of God." As a Christian, Gladys knows it's not nice to say these things, but at her young age, Lucille was an embarrassment—Gladys could not feel any compassion for her.

Then a time came when the family moved a few miles away to Battle Creek, where the school was bigger. Lucille now needed greater assistance because she couldn't navigate the halls. This necessitated she learn to use a wheelchair, and Gladys no longer had to be the helper.

Prior to this change, Gladys only experienced one act of compassion from her parents. Her father, whom she adored, bought her a pair of roller skates. Her mother was furious with him.

"Oh, I was joyous," she said with a slight grin. "Lucille couldn't use them."

Years later, she could see there was a method to her father's madness in purchasing something only she could use.

"I skated day and night," she said.

She was thirteen or fourteen at the time and remembers this as the best thing that happened to her in her childhood, save a few square dances in a relative's home, where the carpet would be rolled back, and she could dance with her cousins.

Gladys describes her mother as quiet and reserved, a nice person, with whom she never established warm feelings. She does not begrudge her mother for wanting things for her disabled daughter.

"I think she paid way too much attention to Lucille. It was one of those things; she may have felt responsible for Lucille's condition."

School Years

Not only was Gladys's home life distressing, so was school.

"Oh, I hated school. I was so bashful that my face would be bright red (matching her hair) if anyone looked at me. I feared that someone would say 'Hi' to me."

In fact, she purposely avoided going into the lunchroom because she had no friends and refused to enter the room by herself.

"I ran over a mile home from school on my lunch hour where my mother would have lunch on the table. I had to eat quickly and run back to school before the lunch was over."

She lived in fear of the time the teacher would call attention to her in class. In fact, she would answer questions as quickly as possible, right or wrong, just so the teacher would call on someone else. She couldn't wait to quit school and get a job—that is exactly what she did. In the second semester of her junior year, at the age of sixteen, she left school and took a job as a nanny and housekeeper for twenty-five cents a week.

"I cleaned house, washed clothes, hung them on the clothesline, and took care of the children. Then, someone offered me fifty cents a week. That was good money. I was able to buy all of my clothes."

As she got older, she became more confident, and her bashfulness became less of a problem.

Marriage and Children: When All the Choices are Bad

As a young woman, Gladys met Stuart John Deland, her future husband. They dated for a while, had fun, and thought they were in love. They married when Gladys was twenty-one, and she gave birth to a son, Stuart, before her husband went into the service during World War II. His checks were sent home.

When he returned, her life became a living hell. She had one child after another—four in five years. Stuart drank up all of his pay and became physically abusive, at times locking her out in the cold.

"People judged me for continuing to have children with this drunken, awful man, but the alternative was getting beat up."

She had no place to go and no way to stop the pregnancies. While the children would later learn that their father was an intelligent man and the best welder around, the bottle took precedence over everything else.

"He was a drinker, and we went hungry," Sharon said.

One time, one of Gladys's sons said to her, "Momma, maybe if I take a big drink of water, I'll feel fuller."

Even seventy-five years later, tears well up as she tells this story.

Another time she spread a blanket on the floor, and one potato was cut into five pieces for the children. It was all they had.

The house was pitiful, too, more like a shack on a back lot—where you could see daylight through the walls and ground through the floorboards. Gladys tacked cardboard on the walls to keep the elements out.

Title IV of the Social Security Act of 1935 included Aid to Dependent Children (ADC). However, all attention was on widows because of losses in World War I and II. While ADC became an integral part of social safety net provisions, the provisions initially covered mothers abandoned or whose husbands were unable to work. Gladys had a husband who worked but drank up all the money.

As ADC expanded, Gladys was able to get a small amount of government financial support for her children. But she used some that was left after groceries to buy a small TV for the children, and the agency terminated her award.

Gladys had to go to work. She found her first good job at Kellogg Company, a company created to promote healthy living. Kellogg Company, Battle Creek, Michigan, began in 1906, after a run as the Battle Creek Toasted Corn Flake Company. Will Keith Kellogg, better known as W.K. Kellogg, at an early age committed himself to good nutrition. He was a Seventh-day Adventist and became a vegetarian, following his religious principles. He and his brother had developed flaked foods, some of the first cold cereal of the day. He began the manufacture of corn flakes at the Battle Creek factory.

Kellogg's was good to employee families. Gladys's daughters, Sharon and Charlotte, remember parties at the plant where the kids were taken on a small train into the auditorium and given a box with candies and cereal. Will Kellogg believed in people. Even during the Depression, he kept the plant going by cutting back hours and adding a fourth shift so that more workers stayed working six hours a day. He created the Kellogg Foundation in the 1930s so he "could invest his profits in people." His company's legendary philanthropy continues today.

Gladys lived a good distance from Battle Creek, and the only job openings were on the third shift from 12:00 a.m. to 6:00 a.m. The plan was for her husband to come home and watch the children while she worked—but he never followed the plan, arriving home long after the bars closed.

On July 7, 1947, Gladys began her first night of work, walking more than a mile through country darkness into the city of Battle Creek. Even though there were streetlights once she reached the city, she walked through slum neighborhoods with trepidation. In spite of this fear, she never had a problem.

Her children were good, too, though they were left alone many hours; her overriding compulsion was to feed her family. She knows she took a big chance, but her kids stepped up and took care of themselves.

"If this had happened today, the children would have been taken away from me. I know that," she says.

The ultimate result of her job with Kellogg, however, was that it allowed her to leave Stuart. With five children in tow, she never looked back, even though they had to live for a short time in a canvas tent at a friend's farm. It was late August, with chilly nights, and they hoisted the food high off the ground to keep the rats from eating it. She eventually was able to save enough money so they could get a place of their own.

After she moved out, Gladys learned where some of Stuart's money had gone, other than for drink. He had fathered other children during their marriage.

"I stuck it out eight years—seven and one-half of those years were pretty bad."

Over the rest of his life, Stuart lived where he could, including the Battle Creek Rescue Mission, where he died at the age of fifty-two.

Middle Years

After Gladys got her own place, family health concerns surfaced. Her mother had died of cervical cancer in her forties, and her father suffered a stroke. Gladys tried to take care of her father, grandfather, and a sister, as well as her five children at home. But her father was bedridden with paralysis and needed more care than she and her children could provide. None of her siblings would pitch in to help.

Finally, she had to put her father into a nursing home in Marshall, twelve miles away. Because she still did not have a car, Gladys and her two daughters walked twenty-four miles round-trip to the facility on weekends.

"He gave up when he had that stroke. Over time, he withered away so he was barely recognizable."

But even these family health issues were not going to be the end of major challenges in Gladys's life. In 1961, Gladys's youngest child, Sharon, at the age of fifteen, developed cancer in her left leg, resulting in an above-the-knee amputation.

Gladys was still working for Kellogg Company, and the nearest reputable hospital for cancer treatment was at the University of Michigan Hospital in Ann Arbor, Michigan, eighty miles away. Every day without fail, Gladys, now owning a car, would make the 160-mile round-trip, come home, try to get a few hours of sleep, and go to work on the third shift. Not once did Sharon's father come for a hospital visit.

Something had to give—Gladys was exhausted, stressed, and starting to miss work. Even with Kellogg Company's investment in people, it was not enough to save her job. She was fired after twelve years of employment.

A more recent family issue haunts Gladys, too—her son Johnnie's death. He was a General Motors retiree, dying of esophageal cancer, and his wife wouldn't let any of the Deland family members come to see him.

"His brother and sisters couldn't go to see him, either. It's so sad."

"She was a hateful woman, and I didn't want to cause a scene." He was cremated.

After Kellogg, Gladys found her next jobs at those places that exist in small rural towns—a retail fabric store, Kentucky Fried Chicken, a bowling alley/bar, and a bar and restaurant called the Sahara Club and Bar (ten years). She eventually became a Greeter at Meijer, where she checked receipts of customers leaving the store. She worked until macular degeneration diminished her eyesight to such an extent that she couldn't see the small print on the receipts. She treasured all of those jobs because this once extremely bashful girl loved talking to people. She retired in her eighties and began collecting Social Security benefits.

Ten years before her retirement, she and Sharon decided they wanted to live on more land and have animals—big pets. They combined their financial resources and looked for land where they could have a trailer and enjoy the outdoors. They wanted to grow their own crops, plant flowers and trees, and raise some livestock. While most people at this time in their lives look to downsize and live in a home involving less work, Sharon and Gladys relished working the land. At the time, Sharon was fifty and Gladys was seventy-five.

In the small village of Bellevue (pop. 1,280) is a dirt road lined with mailboxes and winding, hilly asphalted driveways leading to ranch houses and trailers. The Deland driveway is wrapped by large pine trees on both sides, which obscure a sloping five-acre front lawn with bushes, plants, and fruit trees.

Attached to the front of the trailer is a screened-in porch and around the back is an added deck. Inside the trailer, a bedroom sits at each end. There is a dining and living room area in the middle, next to a small kitchen. A computer sits on a small desk in the living room, and a green parrot keeps up a steady stream of comments and squawks in his cage at the edge of the dining room table.

"Don't put your finger up there (pointing to the cage), he bites," said Gladys.

The Deland women do not shy away from hard physical labor. They did most of the work to improve their twenty-one-acre property. They built their own septic field—finally getting approval after three tries—and a pole barn, with help from Sharon's brother Stan. Next they put in another barn, whose roof Sharon helped shingle. This one would contain their turkeys and laying hens. They also hand-dug holes for fifty fence posts to enclose a pasture for a Tennessee Walker horse and a mule they named Lady Luck.

The free-range laying hens are a story unto themselves. Sharon spent seventy-five dollars per month to feed them.

"There are cheaper foods, but, I buy organic food because I want organic chickens."

The free rangers are picky eaters. Sharon feeds them outdated vegetables the grocery store in town can no longer use.

"But the chickens will not eat the potatoes. Their favorite food, bar none, is popcorn.

They come hotfooting it toward me when I shake that bag—they go crazy." The turkeys loved popcorn, too.

The Delands could host their own farmer's market. They have raised-bed and stock-tank vegetable gardens that produce cauliflower, carrots, broccoli, Brussels sprouts, beets, chard, green beans, and squash. They buy hogs and cows to be butchered, and they sell the eggs from their hens.

Injury and Parts Replacement

Gladys did not use a walker until she was almost ninety. But over the years, she has had a number of parts replaced. In the summer of 2017, Gladys, at the age of ninety-eight, had her knee done. All went well for a while until the knee swelled up like a balloon, prohibiting any weight-bearing. She had a blood clot, and the doctors said it would dissolve by itself, but she had to move; there was nothing more they could do. A week later, she was fine.

"She's up ironing. She's a tough old bird," Sharon said.

In addition to the knee, she's had both hips and a rotator cuff replaced. Then there were the elbow fractures, and a heart attack, after which the doctors installed a pacemaker (twenty-five years ago). Cancer has not reared its ugly head—for her. But four out of five children have had cancer, and four are still alive.

Sharon is a big impetus for their trips to the fitness center, especially on days Gladys would rather stay home. Sometimes, Gladys thinks that Sharon is being mean when she forces the issue of going. But Sharon has a very practical reason for coming and bringing her mother.

"We like to keep our muscles strong. If we don't come here, we would not be able to get around. Then, what would we do with our property?"

"Tell people I am alive because I'm too mean to die," Gladys chuckles.

She still has her sense of humor, and she is not ready to die—not by a long shot. She speaks of people she knows who are in their seventies and have given up.

"They are not sick. They just think seventy is old. They sit on the couch and eat snacks." Gladys can't relate. She is like a swimmer in Lake Michigan. During calm times, she moves gracefully. But when there's stormy weather and forward progress becomes difficult, she uses her invisible life jacket—her sheer determination to keep going and unwillingness to stop trying. For every time she goes under, by God, she's going to bob right back up.

Spreading Their Feathers

Gladys and Sharon are women with a plan for the rest of their lives. They live simply, eat well, and exercise their bodies. It hasn't always been easy, but they rise above their difficulties because of their positive outlook; they keep their focus forward, push through their hardships toward the future.

What accounts for the strength, sheer mental toughness, and longevity of Gladys "Rusty" Deland? It appears that so much in life is about choice, and she chose a better life for herself and her children. But after learning about the struggles she endured to get there, no one could have predicted her active life today at the age of ninety-eight.

The early years of daughter Sharon's life were not pretty, either, making the active and healthy lifestyle she lives today inspiring. She could have followed in the footsteps of her maternal aunt Lucille, becoming more resentful of her condition as each day went by—she didn't.

One family, two generations—an unfathomable marriage and hungry young children for one and a disabled childhood for the other. Is it possible that resilience derives from exactly this litany of adversity? The answer is yes—if viewed from Sharon's personal lens of how bad her childhood could have been and how they got to where they are today:

"At least we didn't have rickets. It was through hard work that we survived, came out tough, and we feel blessed."

Gladys and Sharon took control over their emotional lives, finding happiness in buying property and building a homestead with vegetable gardens and animals. They continue to eat well and be physically active to remain healthy. But there's one more thing. They derive pleasure from simple things, holding in their hearts little moments of joy, like the sheer delight of prancing turkeys.

For Gladys, there's another motivation too. She breaks out in a big smile when she recounts the reaction of her great-grandchildren in recent telephone conversations:

Grandma, are you still working out?

Yes I am.

Grandma, you're awesome!

— 6 —

CONSTANCE FLETCHER

Photo Credit: Stefanie Koeller

MEETING CONSTANCE
Songbirds and Hawk Feathers

The year was 2015, and I joined an exercise class with a group of regular participants. The scene was a small exercise room with rust-colored walls and dark oak wood floors, with an upholstered bench along a windowed wall, and a full-length mirror on the facing wall. A sign to the right of the mirror from the fire marshall of the town of Sahuarita stated that the capacity of the room was seventeen, a number that was regularly pushed to maximum.

Having attended a plethora of aerobics classes, I can say without hesitation that rarely does one include singing. Songs on a CD player or iPod to go along with stepping onto a platform is the norm. Conversation is muted because of shortness of breath—the most you hear is a grunt.

So it was a pleasant surprise to hear two women behind me break out in two-part harmony when the song, "Elvira," came on the CD player. When the song was over, and we took a break, I turned to them, introduced myself, and congratulated them on their stellar voices. They introduced themselves as Connie (5'8" with short grey hair and a smidgen of blonde, wearing a tank top and shorts) and her partner, a tanned Stephanie (5'3" with short black hair, a black T-shirt, and black knitted capris). Their singing lit up an otherwise grueling class session.

But their vocal talent was not my only surprise that day. I was bending over to straighten my step platform in preparation for the next song, and something caught my eye on Connie's leg—a unique, three-inch tattoo. I didn't want to stare, and the only detail I could see without crouching down to within inches of her leg was the end of a feather.

One day, not long after meeting Connie and Stephanie, as we were waiting outside of the aerobics room for the class ahead of us to vacate, I asked Connie about the tattoo. Other tattoos on women's ankles typically include a flower, a butterfly, a heart, or other small symbol, but hers was different. "Do you want the long version or the short one?" she asked. "I'll settle for the short version—for now," I said. What I learned was a window into Connie's life. I knew I'd be back for the longer version.

The Story of the Tattoo

Connie was teaching music on a Menominee Indian reservation in Wisconsin when she received word that her mother had died at 11:00 a.m. It was November 1, 2000, All Saints Day. Connie drove home and walked out on the deck, overwhelmed with thoughts about her mother's death. As she surveyed the landscape, there sat a hawk on the chain-link fence, not fifteen feet away. They made eye contact.

No hawks had been seen there before, and it came back the next day, too. In fact, "this went on during the entirety of my funeral leave," Connie said. At the end of her leave, she saw a hawk while driving back to the reservation.

Connie believed there was significance to this sighting. She asked one of the elders of the tribe to explain its meaning. "This is your mother's presence," said Elder Lillian Nelson. She will continue to be there until she knows you are all right, and then you will see her less often." Connie would "see the hawk every single day for some time."

"When my father, Don, died, lo and behold, here comes an eagle," she exclaimed. The eagle is the highest flying bird on the planet, and its feather represents the highest honor to be bestowed in the American Indian community. According to Indian culture, only Indians can wear eagle feathers, unless an eagle feather is given by an Indian to a non-native.

"Your father is watching out for you. When he thinks you are okay, then the eagle will go away. You must have been close to your father," Lillian said.

She was right. "When I was younger, my dad and I would walk our Wisconsin summer property up north and pick up bird feathers," Connie said.

After her father's funeral, Connie saw the eagle less and less, but she continued to see eagle feathers. When she did, she knew "Pa was here."

Connie took all of this as a sign and knew what she had to do. In 2013, she got a three-inch tattoo, two inches above her right ankle bone. "I decided to get a tattoo with a hawk feather and the eagle fluff (not feather), and rainbow colors on beads on a tendril as the symbol of gay pride. It makes me feel secure and loved, and I've never for a millisecond regretted getting it."

Connie is a woman who straddled two cultures in her career—a herculean feat at times. But as becomes evident from her profile, she did not simply walk between two cultures, she merged the two with a permanent symbol of who she had been and who she has become. Her story follows.

CONSTANCE FLETCHER:
ROOTED IN HER VALUES

Music in Her Bones

"As soon as I could talk, I sang." Constance Fletcher never remembers a time without music in her life.

She was born in 1950 in northern Illinois into a musical family steeped in Catholicism. Her parents were musicians who used to sing around the piano at home. She carried that with her to school, taking private singing lessons with Sister Donna when she was six. "I knew I wanted to be a music teacher early," Connie said.

In fact, she learned to love all kinds of music. "I learned opera from my older sister and was passionate about it from day one."

The music tradition extended beyond her immediate family to aunts and uncles. A cousin was a music teacher at Alverno College, a private Catholic college in Milwaukee.

"She would take me along with her, and I would sing for the nuns," Connie said. During the summer, her family went to a cabin in north central Wisconsin, and she would discuss her interest in music with one of the priests.

When she went to Northern Illinois University, her college music teacher said she had a good chance of joining the Chicago Lyric Opera. "At the age of twenty-one, I took vocal lessons at the Chicago Conservatory of Music costing sixty dollars an hour. But when she was offered a position with the Opera, she turned them down. "They traveled constantly; I am a homebody."

When Connie graduated from Northern Illinois University with a bachelor of science in music education in 1979, she couldn't find a teaching position locally. It was through her priest friend in Wisconsin that she landed her first teaching position. She taught in a Catholic elementary school not far from her family's cottage. But the principal showed little respect for the place of music in the curriculum and allocated few resources. She left.

Her second job was in southeastern Wisconsin in the city of Racine, a middle-class community. Here, she admits, "The kids were great, the parents had money, and this was a good financially supported school." She knew most teachers would die for a teaching position in such a district. But for Connie there was no emotional connection.

"I did not feel fulfilled. Something was missing."

In 1990, the Menominee Indian Tribal Schools, close to her family cottage, broke away from the neighboring Town of Shawno School District to create their own education system, forcing them to hire all new teachers. Connie got a job offer in music education, and she had her choice of grade level. She chose middle and high school. Because it was a new district, she was able to create the music curriculum from scratch.

The Menominee Tribe of Wisconsin

When French fur traders and missionaries first arrived in what is now northern Wisconsin, they met the Menominee people, a tribe of the Algonquin Nation, with whom they formed alliances. But war ensued, as the French, British, and Americans all attempted to lay claim to the land where the Menominee people had lived for as long as they could remember. The Menominees fought but eventually formed treaties with first the French, then the British, and finally the Americans.

There came a time when the United States government attempted to move them west with other tribes, but they refused, instead, preparing for war; they were not moving from the Wolf River area. This was their home where their main sustenance was the rice they harvested, and where they were known as "The Rice People." In the end, the federal government did not force them off the land, and their warriors subsequently fought in the Union army during the Civil War, for the United States in World War I and II, and in all subsequent wars.

Today, the reservation consists of ten townships in three towns: Shawano, Neopit, and Zoar. Approximately three thousand people live on the reservation, which is serviced by a police department, clinics, doctors, dentists, opticians, alcohol and drug rehabilitation, a casino and hotel, a gas station and general store, and a lumber mill, MM Tribal Enterprises.

The First Performance

"They wouldn't come to the front of the room."

The first Christmas concert of the new district occurred in the high school gym on the reservation, with seating for several hundred people. Connie had practiced traditional Christmas songs with her students for most of the fall semester.

First the band played. Then the time came for her students (eight girls and one boy) to rise from their seats and come to the front of the room to sing. Connie had been sitting with her students.

"They all sat there; I looked at them, and they shook their heads, indicating they were not going to come to the front. I had to think quickly.

"If there are any people who would like to sing these Christmas carols, please come and join me or sit where you are and sing," I said.

Several parents came to the front; one student came to the piano with his parent."

Her students progressed to the point where they would sing at the

front of the room, if they could sit on stools. "In the spring concert, they
did come down because they could sit on the stools. I was at the piano,
and they formed a semicircle around the piano. At this time, there were
all girls. They were talented and went on to receive a first place award in
Class A vocal competition among the schools.

"I did not get discouraged. I stayed with them and met them at their
level and gradually brought them up. You have to do this in baby steps.
First singing around the piano, then standing on risers. Through hard
work, dedication, and understanding, they came along. They have to like
you—if they don't like you, they will not learn from you."

Trust was built between teacher and student one day at a time. Once
the students knew they could trust Connie, she began to play many roles
in their lives beyond teacher.

"They used to say I was their mother and counselor first, and then
I was their teacher. In serving these roles, I now felt complete. I got
to know them and their parents. I would chaperone field trips, and my
knowledge of them and their families progressed."

They eventually felt close enough to her to call her "Fletch," their
term of endearment.

Preaching the Gospel of Acceptance of Being Different

Leah Husby started as Connie's music student in middle school. She
originally was scheduled for band, but a friend told her she should switch
to chorus because the teacher was really cool.

Leah rose above the others academically. She became a member of
the National Honor Society and received a scholarship to Beloit College,
a private, distinguished Liberal Arts College in Beloit, Wisconsin.

She was a young woman ahead of her time, encouraging Connie
to read *The Witching Hour* by Anne Rice, and introducing her to Doc

Martin shoes. But like other young people, she was searching for her identity. For a period of time, she experimented with being Goth, the punk-derived subculture, away from her mother's prying eyes.

"Leah would come to school with a backpack and change into her all-black clothes and apply black eyeliner in a small room by my office. Her mother would have had a shitfit if she knew her daughter dressed like that. At the end the day, she would change back to her regular clothes and take off all of the eye makeup."

She often confided in Connie. "There wasn't anything you couldn't come to her with," said Leah. Over time, Connie became a confidante to many students, as the students shared very personal information with her. "I think I'm pregnant," one would say. Connie would set up an appointment at the clinic on the reservation. They came to her with questions about sexually transmitted diseases, too. "I have an itch," one would say. They wanted her advice with things they could not ask their parents.

"I knew the girls who were pregnant needed help. I never judged them. They could come in and tell me anything."

A few of the students were gay or lesbian. Generally, under these circumstances, they would leave the reservation. But they now felt they had someone to talk to. One student, Frannie, came to Connie in tears when her aunt died.

"I need to talk to you about something," she said. "I know what you want to talk about. I know your aunt had a partner," Connie said.

"Many students came out to me. One of my students wanted to jump from the silo and take her own life. We sat down and talked; she changed her mind. Unfortunately, I couldn't save another girl."

"Our reservation tends to be a very private, closed community," Leah said.

"There are some wrong people to share things with. But, there was something about her that was attractive," Leah said.

She came to see Connie's chorus class as the highlight of her day.

"It was a vacation from anxiety for me. I kind of struggled with identity and felt I was an outcast. I dressed differently. But when you know you have unconditional love entering a classroom, how could you not look forward to it."

Connie's warmth and acceptance did not simply extend to her own students. She helped students who weren't in her class with their homework.

"She helped with math, history, and other things. She really reached out to those who were struggling academically," said Leah. Oftentimes, she would ask students to bring in their homework and sit down face-to-face with them before school or in her room at lunch hour. "She was always helping students."

Leah was shy, actually terrified, about singing in front of anyone.

"I was even shy about singing in front of Connie." But Connie took her students to a performance at Bonduel High School, a small rural district off the reservation, where they saw students like them perform, students who showed no qualms about singing in front of hundreds of people. This allowed Connie's students to see possibilities; this was the way they could expand their horizons. On one of the bus rides home, one of Connie's students asked her, "How come we can't do that?"

"We can do that," Connie said.

Between March and May, Connie's students would put their own performance together. "Our final project was to perform in front of a large group of people," Leah said.

Learning New Skills One Step at a Time

Shortly after Connie started teaching, she had a request from the band instructor, who was teaching the boys to sing and drum. He needed

Connie to teach the boys to sing falsetto, a vocal pronation that enables a singer to sing beyond his formal range, in this case, higher range.

"I'll teach them falsetto, but you have to give me two boys for the chorale group and show choir."

"Boys don't sing! Boys drum," one boy said.

This is all they thought they should or could do. Connie knew that, traditionally, males were taught to drum, and this was a very important and revered part of their culture. But was this all they could do? Maybe they could do other things in addition to drumming.

"You guys come and try it for one semester. Get your 'chums' [friends] to try it," Connie said.

They sang beautifully. Then, they wanted Daniel to come into the class; he had the best voice.

One May day at the performing arts center on the reservation, a 1960s medley of Motown music, specifically the song "I Heard It through the Grapevine," was blaring through the speakers. The next year, *Grease* show tunes could be heard.

Bonduel school district high school students, who had been bussed in, sat in the front rows, watching Menominee male and female students dance to their well-choreographed performance. The boys would sing, dance, and swing the girls—sometimes, the girls ending up sitting on their knees.

"They thought this was great!"

The Bonduel students applauded for a long time when the concert ended—something that the Menominee students had never experienced before. But for the Indian boys to be included—it was a first, and it changed some lives. They saw themselves in a different light—adding one more talent to their skill set, even if it was a small one.

Band and choral concerts were held in the evening at the performing arts center. Generally, the band plays on one side of the theatre and chorale on the other, with a sliding accordion wall between them. But at several choral concerts, the wall had to be pulled back because it was standing room only—even the parking lot was at capacity.

"People on the reservation are very community oriented," Leah said. "I like to think of it as a small town times one hundred. These are people who have been here since time immemorial—their roots go back to the beginning."

Leah moved back to the reservation to care for both of her parents, who were diagnosed with cancer. Her father recently died. She sought out Connie's help with this too; they talked about mortality.

The Impact of a Culture of Caring

As Leah reflects on her high school experience, she sees the difference Connie made. "You just don't find that kind of caring in an everyday teacher. It was and is unique to her. She preached the gospel of acceptance tirelessly every day. She saved my life and probably other lives, too."

Connie retired in 2008, but her impact on the lives of more than one generation of Menominees lives. Out of 180 friends on Connie's Facebook page, 155 are her former students.

The students' love of "Fletch" had a profound impact on her, too.

"Teaching there were the best years of my life."

The Importance of the Menominee Forest: A Place of Healing

When people think of Wisconsin as a place, they probably envision dairy cows, cheese, beautiful resort towns in Door County, Madison, the capitol city, surrounded by three lakes, or the Green Bay Packers, Lambeau Field, and loyal fans wearing funny cheeseheads.

But for Connie and the Menominee people in northeast Wisconsin, 45 miles northwest of Green Bay, along Highway 47, their sense of place is the Menominee Forest, over 219,000 acres of pristine trees. According to pilots flying over, it looks like a large rectangle of unsullied green. According to people on the ground, its existence is personal.

It serves many purposes. It is a place where healing takes place. Connie recalls that she would take her students into the forested areas by the falls of the Wolf River, which flows through the reservation, just to talk when they were having difficulties. The forest provided extracurricular activities, such as berry picking, maple syrup making, and, in the dead of winter, sledding.

In addition to spiritual health, the Forest provides economic sustenance for the tribe. Owned by the Menominee Tribe since 1854, the forest consists of thirty species of trees, which are logged at a sawmill on the property, owned and operated by Menominee Tribal Enterprises.

Many students' parents worked for the mill. Such was the case for Leah's father, who was a forester for his entire working life.

Of particular interest, however, is the fact that after 150 years of logging, which ordinarily guts forests, the tribe has managed to have more standing timber volume on the property today than on day one by following their guiding principle of taking care of Mother Earth.

Following the Seventy Generation Principle

The Seventh Generation Principle taught by Native Americans says that in every decision, be it personal, governmental, or corporate, we must consider how it will affect our descendants seven generations into the future. Sustainability in forestry integrates this value of taking care of nature, using only as much as you need, and no more.

The revered Menominee Chief Oshkosh (1795-1858) issued a land ethic statement that said, *take only mature trees, sick trees, and the trees that have fallen*—a practice followed to this day. These practices have received international acclaim and visitors from throughout the world. The basic concept of harvesting timber is to start at one end of the forest and go to the other in such a manner that, when done, the first areas cut would be ready for cutting again. Because of this work, Menominee Tribal Enterprises has received recognition from the United Nations for balancing land use with sustainable practices to preserve forests for future generations—exemplifying the Seventh Generation Principle.

Present and future generations benefit from the Enterprises in other ways, too. The approximate 125 employees are mostly tribal members; an additional 180 workers are employed sporadically throughout the year. In addition, every year in December, employees receive "stumpage," MTE's own version of profit-sharing, similar to the bonuses United Automobile Workers union members receive from the automotive companies every year, the amount varying depending on the company's profit.

Sharing the wealth and the forest—the Menominee way.

Personal Reflections on Connie's Values

I am only one; but still I am one.
I cannot do everything, but still
I can do something; and because I
cannot do everything, I will not
refuse to do the something I can do.
-Edward Everett Hale

Connie worked on an Indian reservation for twenty-eight years and was passionate the entire time. In my mind, this takes some doing. "It fit for me," she said.

Connie's life teaching on the reservation represents a rootedness in service that inspires me. I could not have done it, never wanting to restrict myself to one cause or one place, but touching bases with many. I volunteered in the fields of domestic violence, substance abuse, and women's rights. I could devote my energies and passions for a time—usually, three to seven years—then I would move on. I never stopped caring about these issues, and I continued to contribute to them in other ways. But I could not plant my feet as firmly or for as long as Connie.

I suspect others could or would not do what Connie did either, but for different reasons. Some would see teaching on a reservation as too difficult and, at the first opportunity, move to a better teaching environment. For any middle or high school teacher, challenges loom daily; but on a reservation, I can't help but think students may have more complex needs.

Constance Fletcher stayed at her job because it aligned with her values—personal values learned at home. She was able to impact more than one generation of students, as well as students who might not have graduated without her. Here are the words of Superintendent Wendell Waukau at the time of her exit interview: "...because the kids trusted and liked you, fewer students went into alternative education—they were ready to learn from you."

Many of us want our lives to have meaning—not all succeed. Because of my "time to go" mentality and behavior, the time for me to influence and guide another life has been limited. Connie took the road less traveled, and it made all the difference.

PART III

WALKING AWAY

_7_

CAROL CROCKER HARTON

Photo Credit: Sherry Forrest

MEETING CAROL HARTON

I met and became friends with Carol Harton when I began work at Lansing Community College in the fall of 1993. I had been living in Detroit for more than twenty-five years, watching the community become increasingly African-American. I was in the presence of African Americans most of the time, not simply at work, but in my neighborhood. It was not unusual, then, for me to make African American friends.

Carol and I had many things in common that cemented our friendship. We both had lived in Detroit, she for eighteen years, me for twenty-five. We loved different cultures, beautiful clothes, and jazz. We were both extroverts, studied sociology, and loved people—especially students. We once bought the same scarf for each other as a Christmas present.

In fact, the biggest difference between us became apparent when we traveled for work and shared a hotel room. She stayed up late, and I went to bed early. She would sit inches from the television and turn the volume down late into the night. I, on the other hand, would tiptoe around the room when I rose early the next day so as not to wake her.

How many interracial friendships exist across the country? They seem to be more visible among younger people, in the world of sports and music, in large urban areas, and on the East and West Coasts. But among Midwest small town middle-aged women? Probably not throngs.

Conversations surrounding race and friendship don't come easy. Carol's story is about many things, but it is also a story about simple friendships crossing racial lines.

CAROL ANN CROCKER: QUIET STRENGTH

The only person you are destined to become
is the person you decide to be.
—*Ralph Waldo Emerson*

Carol's Early Years

Physical fights erupted routinely at the Crocker home on Friday nights at 4832 Scotten Street on Detroit's west side, a street of rundown frame houses. On his way home from work, paycheck in hand, Erskine Crocker would stop by the house across the street and drink corn whiskey. By the time he got home, he was sufficiently liquored up to pick a fight with his wife, Druscilla, a big woman who would fight back. Some nights, she would knock the crap out of him, further fueling his rage.

Three Crocker children stood at the ready to break up their parents' fights. Sanderius was the oldest, Carol was four years younger, and Sherry was six years younger than Carol. A half-brother to the Crocker children was older and resided in Georgia, the state of Druscilla's and Erskine's upbringing.

Erskine drank all weekend, breaking windows and cutting telephone lines so the police could not be called. Saturday mornings would find all three children and their mother in their barren attic to avoid further trouble. They sat on a mat and listened to the radio. Sanderius had his chemistry set to play with, and Carol would bring a book to read.

The summer heat in the attic was unbearable, but they bore it. During the school year, come Monday morning, Erskine would head back to work hungover, and the Crocker children would head back to school as if nothing of consequence happened over the weekend. In the midst of this traumatic home life, all were good students, with Carol, an avid reader, concentrating on English, history, and social sciences.

Erskine Crocker was not always a bad father. On days of the week when he wasn't drinking, he could be quite pleasant. He would read the *Detroit Free Press* and *The Michigan Chronicle* (the newspaper of the black community), listen to the Tigers on the radio, or watch Cassius Clay (Muhammad Ali) fights.

The Crocker children knew there was something wrong with their mother, too, although she was able to cook, wash clothes, sew, quilt, and attend church. After Sanderius went into the military, the girls would come home from school and find her sitting in her kitchen chair, rocking back and forth in utter silence.

Later in their lives, they were told that their mother had Tourette's syndrome, a disease of motor tics and sometimes assaultive behavior, which was worsened by daily stresses. Friends were never invited to the Crocker home because, in addition to unpredictable parents, they might encounter rats and roaches.

An Escape Route

During the early 1960's, through Title I of the Elementary and Secondary Education Act, the Extended School Program, and the Great Cities Program for School Improvement, the federal government provided funding for services to inner-city school students. These grants provided student tutoring in key academic areas during and after school, supplemental summer instruction, and funds for college scholarships. Carol used these services to prepare herself for college.

A black and white graduation photo from the 1967 Western High School Yearbook *The Beacon* shows Carol as a stern-looking young woman perhaps, reflecting on her hard life. But that was about to change.

After four years on the honor roll, she was ready for college and eligible for a full tuition, room-and-board scholarship at Michigan State University. She was the beneficiary of the college's efforts to achieve a more diverse racial and socioeconomic student body. Faculty from MSU had added their presence to inner-city schools as tutors, and their efforts paid off. While MSU minority scholarships had been available prior to this time, all recipients had come from middle-class communities.

In the 1967 fall semester, Carol was a member of the first group of 159 black students from inner-city schools in Michigan, most from Detroit, out of a total college enrollment of over 25,000. These students would begin their MSU life as members of the Detroit Project. The Project included intensive support services, weekly group meetings and study sessions with a mentor, as well as meetings with counselors. Students in the Project were housed together in dorm rooms.

Carol easily acclimated to dorm life at Acres Hall. Race didn't matter to Carol. She made friends with a couple of white girls across the hall, one of whom was Diana Catallo from a strong Italian Catholic family in Dearborn.

"My room was across the hall from Carol's. I went across the hall to introduce myself to Carol and her roommates. I was from Dearborn, a suburb of Detroit, and didn't know any black people other than the people who came to my father's store in Detroit.

"Carol and I became best friends and did everything together—especially partying. There were four of us, Carol and one of her roommates, and me and my roommate. On the weekends, we would pretty much be together every day," Diana said.

"During that time, they would lock the doors of the dorm, and you couldn't come in after 11:00 p.m. or midnight. We would just stay out all night and go to bars in Lansing.

"During the week, we ate meals together and got in trouble because we made so much noise playing cards and listening to music—we had to go in front of a tribunal."

But Carol relished her sister's visits too, showing her around the beautiful tree-lined campus, framed by the Red Cedar River and eating in the cafeteria. She was particularly pleased to introduce Sherry to new foods.

"I remember one time Carol came home and brought a pizza and a submarine sandwich to show me. 'Look at these,' she exclaimed, as she pointed to them. I don't recall ever going out to eat as a child, not even McDonald's," Sherry said.

But, Carol did not come home much during her college years. When she did come home, tension spilled over between her and her dad, and the yelling started. Druscilla remained silent during these events. Carol thought she was grown and free to do as she pleased, including staying out as late as she wanted.

They had one of their most heated arguments on the weekend in August of 1967 when the Detroit 'uprisings' broke out. Carol wanted to be out on the streets with her friends, and Erskine tried to keep her home, understanding the risk she was taking. Carol was defiant, and she stayed away.

Although the mid-60s were turbulent times on campus with civil rights, Vietnam, and women's rights demonstrations, Carol and her friends did not participate. "We did not get involved in demonstrations. We partied and had a good time," Diana said.

But Carol continued to be compliant with the Detroit Project meetings, studied hard, majoring in sociology, and was able to graduate on time, unlike some of the other Detroit Project students.

New Arrangements

Carol's sister Sherry was in seventh grade when Carol left for college. There came a time when she was living with her paternal aunt Roxy because her mother was in Georgia with her son Eugene. But one year after Carol's graduation in 1971, at the end of Sherry's junior year in high school, this arrangement changed.

Druscilla called Aunt Roxy and said she was on her way home to pack up and take Sherry back down to Georgia with her. Sherry was a junior in high school and thriving. She even lost weight because the stress was gone from her life. Sherry had been a stress eater, following in Carol's footsteps, tipping the scales at over 200 pounds as an elementary student.

But Roxy was afraid of Druscilla and wouldn't challenge her. Sherry was afraid to be in her own home, even for a limited time, with her mother and father.

"He had guns hidden under the house. I knew he would never hurt me, I was his baby. But I could become a casualty in their heated arguments," Sherry said.

She started to have a meltdown. She recalled a heated telephone call between her parents and Carol, and the next thing she knew Carol was headed to Roxy's. She opened Roxy's front door, looked at Sherry, and said "Pack your bags, you are coming to live with me." Her parents were not happy, but did not challenge her.

"While Carol did not talk much about her former life at home, she did talk about Sherry. Sherry became her life, almost like a mother-daughter relationship, even though only six years separated them. Sherry's life was definitely changed by her move to East Lansing," said Diana.

"She was my mother, father, sister, and brother," Sherry says of Carol.

One woman—many roles. In the five-person Crocker family unit, Carol and Sherry remained the only fully functioning, healthy adults.

Brother Sanderius had gone off to Vietnam when Carol started high school. But between a violent childhood and hate for his father, alcohol, and post-Vietnam Post Traumatic Stress Disorder (PTSD), the Sanderius who came home was only a ghost of the brother they remembered— the smart one who got As in Latin at Chadsey High School.

During all of Carol and Sherry's adult lives, Sanderius lived in Detroit, either on the streets or in homeless shelters. For over thirty years, although they tried a few times through different means to find him, they assumed he had died on one of those streets.

Building a New Family and Life

Sherry finished her final year at East Lansing High School and spoke at graduation. Then, it was her turn to attend MSU. Thereafter, the two put down roots in the Lansing area and began their new lives there. Though they were going to live in an area with a small black community compared to Detroit, this was not a determining factor.

"I don't think color mattered to Carol. She liked people for who they were," Diana said.

Lansing is where their adult lives would flourish, even though the rest of their family's wouldn't. In 1979, Carol and Sherry received word that their father was found frozen to death on a Detroit street. Druscilla had permanently moved to Georgia to live with her minister son and had sporadic telephone contact with her daughters. Sanderius might be dead or alive, for all they knew.

In 1980, when Carol was thirty-two, she met her future husband at the Black and Tan, a bar that had a predominantly black clientele in Lansing. Larry could be described as a "high roller" and was quite the charmer, a decade older than Carol, living in Chicago 250 miles away, and a long-tenured employee of the US Department of Agriculture.

Larry wasn't going to walk away from his job, but, Carol wasn't going to move to Chicago and leave her sister, either. She preferred the small community. So, in the end, they became one of the many professional couples who lived separately and spent some weekends together every month, driving four hours to see each other. Christopher Jonathan Edward Harton was born three years into the marriage in October, 1983.

Christopher's birth would change the dynamics of the long-distance marriage, with Carol not driving to Chicago as often on the weekends because of her son's activities, which corresponded with her sister's family's activities. She provided a safe and happy home life for her son in south Lansing, unlike the one she experienced. While she often admitted she might be spoiling him, buying him things he wanted, she was no pushover—having high expectations for him, emphasizing the importance of educational achievement.

Carol herself was the beneficiary of her husband's many gifts. Larry loved nice clothes, always dressed sharp, and drove Cadillacs. He would send Carol beautiful clothes in boxes from Chicago. These boxes would arrive at the office, and women would stand around her desk, watching the grand opening, "oohing and aahing." Carol was an attractive woman who loved beautiful clothes and dressed accordingly.

Over the years, Christopher only remembers going to Chicago a few times to buy school clothes. When his father came to the Lansing home on periodic weekends, he remembers arguments and tension. He also remembers when his father was supposed to come and didn't, like his high school graduation.

Carol never talked about her reasons for marrying Larry with anyone but her sister. She married one year after Sherry. Perhaps, she married for the same reasons as others. Perhaps, it was something she felt compelled to do to become a mother, being over thirty at the time. Perhaps, the relationship changed substantially when their son was born.

One of Carol's colleagues distinctly remembers that she "avoided discussion of her marriage like the plague." Whatever happened, she chose not to talk about their relationship with her son. Carol and Larry would eventually divorce after nineteen years of marriage.

But it would be a mistake to think Christopher was deprived of a male role model all those years. He had his uncle Ted and a minister at his church who took up the slack and took him under their wings.

Finding Her Career Passion

In 1987, Carol was recruited by then-president of Lansing Community College, its first African American, to teach part-time in the criminal justice program. She was the perfect candidate to teach future corrections officers about the corrections system. She could tell real stories, because she had worked with the probation department and at a methadone clinic, about what happens behind bars and once inmates leave prison behind.

This particular period in US history, the 1990s, represented a time with an increasing emphasis on incarceration and a corresponding need to increase corrections officers. New Michigan legislation made it mandatory for state corrections officers to receive fifteen college credits prior to employment. More community college faculty would be needed to accommodate these students, and Carol was encouraged to and applied for a full-time faculty position at the college.

She got the job, and it represented a turning point for her, beginning a career in which she would use all of her talent, passion, and skills to help people embrace educational opportunities as she had done. She was a popular teacher, always approachable, and the students of color saw in her a role model.

But she was no pushover here either, using the same tough love she proffered with her son. When she was sharing her disappointment in a student's performance, somewhere in the conversation were the words, "Look, this is exactly what you need to do," pointing to the poor behavior rather than to the person.

Carol later returned to college to get a master's degree in adult and continuing education. Decades later she would share with her coworkers the guilt she felt because of her college success and lament the fact that some of the others from Detroit who started with her were not successful.

The Education Imperative: Generation Two

Carol was devoted to having Christopher be a successful student. But there came a time in third grade when Carol was notified by Christopher's third-grade teacher that he was acting up in the classroom and stood a chance of being held back. She mentioned something about his immaturity. Carol's response was swift and measured. For the next several weeks in that classroom, there sat Carol in a chair next to her son. She knew what it took, and he got the message.

Another school crisis occurred when Christopher was in middle school. He came home from school one day and told his mother he needed to change schools. He was going to a school where there were a lot of fights and too many distractions in the classroom. He felt the school wasn't working for him.

Carol again acted with lightning speed. She knew about school choice and was in a position to try to get Christopher into a different school system, one that concentrated on academics. One of the better school systems in the area had a lottery, Christopher had cousins in that system, and his uncle was able to run interference for him.

Christopher started eighth grade in the new district, at first struggling because the expected academic performance level was so much higher. Following in his mother's footsteps, he got the help he needed, and when he started high school, he was prepared.

But Carol still monitored his school performance. Homework came before anything else when Christopher got home from school—before friends and sports. One evening when she finished a particularly late meeting at the college, she mentioned that her day was not over yet. "I still have to go home and check Christopher's homework," she said.

Friendship and Race

Christopher could be described as a typical boy, loving sports, actively participating in football and basketball, working out at the YMCA, and faithfully watching University of Michigan football games with his uncle Ted. But Carol wanted him to learn golf.

Indian Hills Golf Course is a small nine-hole, par-three golf course in Okemos, Michigan, a small suburb of Lansing named after Ojibwe Chief Okemos. In the mid-1990s, a ragtag group of twelve middle-aged women formed a pseudo golf league. Most of the members worked at Lansing Community College, but some were neighbors and friends. One of the rules for this informal group of golfers was that members had to be mediocre to poor golfers. Players were mostly novices who played a scramble, able to use the team's best ball on each hole.

Carol asked if Christopher could join the group to learn the game, and he was welcomed. While he was a novice and learning like everyone else, when he connected with the ball, it soared. His was usually the best ball on his team, and his team usually won the scramble.

At first, staff at the clubhouse looked at the group as rather odd, twelve middle-aged mostly white women and one black adolescent playing a round of golf at a predominantly white golf course. But for the team members who knew Carol, they saw it as par for the course, so to speak. Christopher saw it as a chance to learn a new skill and wasn't bothered by who his teammates were. He does remember he and his mother being the only minorities there.

Chris and his golf partners acted like old friends. Plenty of banter and teasing went on, no different than other golfers. But one of the women was unforgettable. She took an inordinate amount of time to tee up, particularly after she received a very expensive set of golf clubs as a gift from her father. It was painful for Christopher to watch and wait for her on each hole—his facial expressions exhibited extreme anguish. But the pain was shared by all.

The experience did not turn him away from golf. "I haven't improved much, but I still love being out on the course," he says. While most young men Christopher's age, perhaps most particularly young black men, would rather die than hang out with their mother and her friends, Christopher saw it as nothing out of the ordinary.

But his love of golf did come as a surprise to some of his new white classmates when he started at Okemos High School.

"This white guy was talking about golf, and I chimed in and said, 'I love golf.' The astonishment registered on this guy's face. 'You play golf?' I later heard through the grapevine that he was telling his white friends, 'Hey, there's this black guy here at school who plays golf!'"

The End to an Otherwise Ordinary Journey

On August 3, 2009, Carol and her sister were in their regular exercise class together at the YMCA in downtown Lansing. They were lying on a mat on the floor, holding a large exercise ball, first over their head and then bending up to take it to their toes.

Carol had just got off her cellphone, talking with Christopher about dinner. Sherry finished performing the routine, pulling herself up from the prone position and touching her toes with the ball. She looked over at Carol, who did not get up. Sherry started talking to Carol to ask her if anything was wrong, moving in her direction. Carol's eyes were rolled back in her head. Sherry screamed, and a paramedic in the room called for an ambulance. Sherry in the meantime called Christopher and ran to her husband who was working out in another room. They all rushed to the hospital behind the ambulance.

Carol was in a coma, and her condition was grave. She had experienced a stage 5 cerebral aneurysm, the worst kind. Doctors put a tube in her head to relieve the swelling. Neurologists argued about whether she should be taken to another hospital with more advanced life support. But it was sixty miles away, and one doctor didn't think she would make it. Others came to the hospital to wait, including Christopher's father and friends from work and golf friends.

Within a day, she had another bleed—all hope was gone. Christopher's anger and sorrow overwhelmed. He threw his iPhone against the wall.

At the age of twenty-five, he had to make the decision to pull the plug. Carol's life ended at the age of fifty-nine.

On September 4, 2009, the pews at Friendship Baptist Church on the south side of Lansing, were filled to capacity. Over a thousand people, including Christopher's former fraternity brothers and friends from Western Michigan University in Kalamazoo, sixty miles away, sat shoulder to shoulder. Some of the fraternity brothers had been guests in the Harton home and knew of the special bond between Carol and Christopher.

People of every race, religion, and creed paid their respects. One by one, they rose to give testimony to Carol's influence on their lives. One by one they rose to attest to Carol's friendship, helping them through difficult times. Christopher said he was stunned to hear how much his mother meant to others. Reverend Lester Stone had to finally cut off the testimonials, the service having already lasted over two hours.

A Life of Influence

Christopher heard a lot he didn't know about his mother's work at the time of her death. People from every corner of the community, people that she supervised as a probation officer, and students she helped at Lansing Community College approached him at the funeral home. They told him that Carol had turned their lives around, away from a life of crime. Others said because of her counseling, they stayed in college.

But the tributes did not end when Carol died. Seven years after her death, her name still sits to honor her legacy in four distinct places in the Lansing community. Lansing Community College began a new scholarship fund in her name, in recognition of her love for and support of thousands of students.

Every year, she had worked with the college's foundation, its fundraising arm, through her participation in an annual lip-sync talent show, dressing up and singing songs of The Supremes, raising money for student scholarships. A resolution praising her work is part of the official record of the LCC Board of Trustees.

Antioch, a small nondenominational church in Lansing, continues an annual 5K race, with team awards in Carol's name for those who bring the most participants to the race. Those middle-aged golf friends honored her as well. On the perimeter of Hole 4, at the Indian Hills Golf Course, sits a seven-year-old Ginkgo tree, the oldest species of tree in the world, known for its perseverance. Under it sits a plaque that reads: *In memory of Carol Harton: our friend and golf buddy.*

— 8 —

BILLIE PASE QUALTROUGH

Photo Credit: Nancy Paepke

MEETING BILLIE

I went to jail once, courtesy of the Mormon Governor of Michigan, George Wilcken Romney. The year was 1968, the month was April, and Martin Luther King had just been assassinated. Fearing civil unrest like that of the 1967 uprisings in Detroit, Governor Romney issued an Emergency Proclamation stating that no more than three people could publicly gather.

At the time, I belonged to a social justice group called People Against Racism (PAR), whose mission was to educate people about racism and promote racial equality. Leaders of PAR decided to defy the order and demonstrate against the racism that killed Martin Luther King Jr., with full knowledge of the illegality of this action. Members could choose to march or not. I was in.

At the time, all I knew about the Governor was that he was a Republican and a Mormon. I had a distinct impression that the Mormon denomination was different in principle and practice from other Christian denominations, but I didn't know any specifics.

As a passionate, uninformed twenty-one-year-old, I assumed that the Governor did not possess strong beliefs supporting equal rights. I was mistaken. Romney, in fact, held strong beliefs about equal rights for African Americans and had himself marched with Martin Luther King Jr. down Woodward Avenue and campaigned for open housing in Detroit. Not only that, as a result of his open support for fair housing laws and equal rights, he received hate mail from other Mormons.

I eventually left Michigan, as did the Romney family when George became the secretary of housing and urban development in the Nixon administration. He returned to Michigan after Nixon's first term.

Over the ensuing years, I picked up bits and pieces of Mormon history because I was curious. In 2005, when I was traveling across Illinois, I saw a brief glimpse into the Mormon Midwest journey of Prophet Joseph Smith and his followers when I passed through the town of Nauvoo. No Mormons, to my knowledge, crossed my path throughout my working life.

In 2015, I began researching my maternal ancestry. I was directed to the Family History Center in East Lansing, Michigan, twenty miles from my home. I knew nothing about this center but was grateful it sponsored an annual seminar on family genealogy.

In one session, I found myself in a small seminar room with twenty chairs packed in close. When the speaker asked how many had conducted genealogy research on their ancestors, everyone raised their hand but me. Then the speaker asked how many in the room were Mormon? Again, everyone raised their hand but me. I was startled. How was it that I ended up in a room with all Mormons who were so intent on researching their ancestors?

At home, I reflected on this situation. I had learned that the public and historical records in the archives of the Church of Jesus Christ of Latter-day Saints in Utah were the most comprehensive in the United States, if not the world. Perhaps, there was the connection between the existence of this large body of knowledge and Mormons utilizing it to conduct genealogical research. But why were they doing this?

In 2016, I met Billie Louise Qualtrough in Sahuarita, Arizona, a small town south of Tucson, where I was spending my winters in retirement. Billie was the instructor in one of my aerobics classes. In conversation, she stated that she had been in a band and that she retired as an engineer—such a good use of both right and left-brain in music and math, I thought.

From other women in the class, I learned there was more to Billie's life than aerobics, music, and science. Not only had Billie been a Mormon, but she had left the faith and shared her experience on a YouTube video entitled *The Ex Mormon Files,* hosted by Earl Erskine.

Watching the video only confirmed my dearth of knowledge about Mormons; I knew more about Buddhists. I had many questions, but the central one was about the journey of her Mormon family to Arizona. Arizonians know there are many Mormons in their state because of its proximity to Utah. However, as a midwesterner, I was new to this regional geography.

Meeting Billie was serendipitous—an antidote to my ignorance. I shared with her that I was writing a book about ordinary women who had uncommon lives, and she consented to an interview. I reminded her that people in our small retirement community might read her story.

"I have nothing to hide."

She started with her maternal family's trek to the White Mountains in Arizona in the mid-1880s.

The Mormon Journey to the Mountaintop

The history of the Mormon trek across the Plains in the mid-1880s is a tale of woe, with suspicion, religious persecution, discrimination, and acts of violence following them until their eventual settlement in Utah. Doubt about their true Christianity was always present because of their practice of men having several wives.

In 1839, a Mormon settlement built their first temple outside of New York in the central Illinois town (then a territory) of Nauvoo. But after five years, Prophet Joseph Smith and his brother were jailed for inciting a riot, and a mob stormed the jail, killing the Smiths. Brigham Young, the new Mormon leader, hearing rumors of more violence against his members, quickly began a journey westward. Three thousand exiled Mormons left Nauvoo in five hundred wagons.

Young's plan was to get to Omaha, Nebraska in four to six weeks, but because of the rain and ensuing mud and swollen rivers, the trip took sixteen weeks. Young and Billie's grandfather eventually arrived at the basin of the Salt Lake Valley.

But the Mormon practice of polygamy continued to be a problem. The federal government would pass a statute and a change in church doctrine would eventually ban the practice of plural marriages.

When Young ended his term as governor of the Utah Territory, he concentrated his efforts on expanding Mormon settlements, requesting the elders to take their families across the White Mountains into northern Arizona. The journey was treacherous and a true test of Mormon faith and perseverance, as each animal had to be lowered by rope down the mountain. Challenges would continue, as Apaches and people of Mexican descent had been living in the area long before and did not welcome their arrival.

Some of the families who arrived in White Mountain towns became ranchers, raising sheep and cattle, acquiring great wealth. But some struggled as subsistence farmers whose existence was harsh. Such was the plight of one family arriving in the town of Eagar—the Wiltbanks. While they never went hungry, growing vegetables and keeping them in a root cellar so they would last longer, they had little in the way of clothing and worldly possessions. The class distinction between them and the cattle rancher families couldn't have been starker.

As a child, Billie's mother, Charleen Fay Wiltbank,, went barefoot much of the time because she did not want to wear out the one pair of shoes she had for church and school. She lived this meager, hard, devout Mormon life feeling inferior. Even though she was raised with values of love and kindness for the poor, needy, and the afflicted, she herself was victimized by other Mormon children and made to feel an outcast in her own town. Even so, this is where she stayed, dying in the home of her birth in 2016.

It is in this small Mormon town of Eagar that Billie Louise Pase Qualtrough has her strongest childhood memories.

BILLIE PASE QUALTROUGH:
A JOURNEY FROM HAPPINESS TO HELL AND BACK

The Checklist

In 1975, Billie Louise Pase, twenty-one years old, began a promising romantic relationship with David. She thought back to the list from her training in the Church of Jesus Christ of Latter-day Saints (LDS), attributes memorized by girls and young women in preparation for choosing the right Mormon husband: a man who had completed a mission, a man who attended church regularly, a man who would raise his family in the Church, and a man who tithes and is otherwise temple-worthy. In her mind, she could place a check next to each item.

Billie had only known David for three months. But he reminded her of her father.

"He was physically strong, very bright, and my image of a superhero —a vision of everything that was good in my father." She could not talk to her parents about the relationship, as her parents were in South Africa for her father's work. She relied on what she had learned in the Church and proceeded with wedding plans to marry in the temple. First, they scheduled their Worthiness Interview, in which they attested to their adherence to the Code of Health by abstaining from premarital sex, alcohol, tobacco, and coffee, among other things.

Billie had known the Mesa temple where they would marry her whole life. It was the first to be built in Arizona in 1919 and was dedicated on October 23, 1927. Its construction intentionally resembled the temples of Jerusalem.

Billie and David were married by a civilian administrative president who presided over the temple. The LDS marriage ceremony is called a sealing ordinance, and children born or adopted into such eternal marriages can also be sealed to their families forever. A temple marriage is the only way a husband and wife can be "sealed in eternity." Sealed families will have a subsequent life after their earthly life.

Unlike marriages that last only "til death do you part,'" temple sealings ensure that death cannot separate loved ones. Those sealed know that marriage is their most cherished earthly relationship next to their relationship with the Lord. The one way a woman can achieve salvation and exaltation (becoming more godlike) is through marrying a righteous man. Billie was sure she was doing that.

Only temple-worthy people are allowed to physically enter the temple, so the wedding was small, with only eighteen other Mormons in attendance.

Within months of the wedding, she knew she had made a mistake.

A Mormon Childhood

Billie found joy in the Mormon community into which she was born in 1954. She was raised in Mesa during the winters and in the mountain community of Eagar, Arizona (elevation 7,000 ft.), during the summers. At the time, Eagar was 99 percent Mormon and Mesa was 85 percent Mormon.

Billie's mother was a died-in-the-wool Mormon. Her father, a botanist, converted to Mormonism to please his wife. Their marriage was sealed in the same Mesa temple as Billie's would be. Billie adored her father, who, as a Forest Service scientist, took measurements in the forest to see if there was enough grass to support grazing livestock. Consequently, she was exposed in her daily life to things and ideas from a scientific perspective.

"As a young person, I did everything I was supposed to do. The Church is all-encompassing and takes over every aspect of your life. You do everything with other Mormons. It can be limiting, but if you do not challenge the status quo, it works."

Billie's mother had been raised with country music and played the piano, so Billie's musical life began at the age of seven when her mother had her join the choir. Strong support for the arts, dance competitions, plays, road shows, and talent shows existed in the community—most of the time. There was one big exception: when Billie's family, and a few other brave Mormons, decided to produce a fully-clothed version of the rock musical *Hair*.

"I had a gay cousin who was studying theatre in Los Angeles and had been working in children's theatre. He was in his twenties, and I was fourteen. He came back to Springerville, a predominantly Catholic Mexican community adjacent to Eagar to do the production. I got the female lead, mostly because there weren't very many people older than me who could sing or dance."

The year was 1969, and the play was antiwar and dealt with other controversial issues of the day. There was a town hall meeting before the play. Even with the actors fully clothed, the production was highly controversial because of the content.

"I remember people from the cast handing out flowers; we were the flower children."

The bishop of the Mormon church told his congregation they should not attend the production; the Catholics in Springerville were not thrilled about it, either. So, the attendance was small.

"Even though we were ostracized for participating, the resentment eventually blew over."

"My childhood was the perfect environment for all aspects of the performing arts. It formed my personality, and I have great gratitude and joy for what my family and the Church gave me.

"In fact, I started a rock band at the age of fourteen and stayed until I was eighteen, playing keyboard and an electric synthesizer. Music would continue to be an important part of my adult life."

Nature and animals brought Billie happiness, too. During the summer, when the family spent time at the base of the White Mountains, Billie would work for a couple of hours at home, and then her mother would allow her and her siblings to disappear.

"I fancied myself a female Tarzan—running wild. Sometimes, we would rent grazing animals so we could have animals. I had Sam-the-Donkey, a retired rodeo donkey. If he didn't want to do something, he would duck his head down. I would try to get him to ride me as a passenger, and he wouldn't do it. I would whack him with an umbrella.

"I loved Sam so much, I dressed in a white veil, and we had a small wedding ceremony out in the orchard, with my mother in attendance. She laughed and teased me about having 'a jackass of a husband.'"

Tragedy struck when Billie was in sixth grade, and her aunt, a mother of nine, died in her forties. Billie's mom took in those children still at home. Billie already had three siblings: an older sister, a younger sister, and a younger brother. To this number, now six more would be added.

"The rule was that all the kids were welcome. My mom was cooking and feeding us all the time. Her work was constant."

"When my cousins moved in, I was in sixth grade, and my grades tanked. I became very distracted. I couldn't get my homework done, there were so many people in the house."

Billie recalls the scene of the whole group going to church.

"We came into the church from the back and walked in a row to the front, taking up an entire pew."

Each of Billie's siblings began to have issues at home. Billie's father's way of dealing with the stress at home was to stay away.

"He didn't want to have conflict, and he was away a lot."

Billie's parents would eventually divorce.

Becoming the Perfect Woman

After high school graduation and a brief time overseas, Billie enrolled at Brigham Young University where she experienced a disastrous first year. Because she had been so distracted during her high school and middle school years as a result of her chaotic home environment, she never learned the discipline necessary to succeed in college. Even though she received good grades in high school, once she was on her own, she could not muster what it took to get those same grades in college. But that wasn't all.

"I was an outcast in every way. I majored in police science—not a good thing for a Mormon woman. But it made sense to me. I was the kid who was playing army games as a child. I was the leader of everything—Captain Kirk was me.

"I was supposed to comply with the image of a perfect woman."

Her first-year college experience was a total disillusionment in another way too. Billie had a roommate who was overweight, but she was the perfect Mormon woman. One day they walked down to the cafeteria and observed "the returned missionary men rating the women on their looks, including my roommate—it was disgusting to me."

"Mormons are supposed to be about love, kindness, respect, and women are protected and special. What I experienced was a far cry from this.

"I left college after the first year."

She simply did not fit the mold.

Righting Yourself in a Wrong Marriage

Billie's husband David was a very powerful man in the Church. He was charismatic and perfect on the surface—after all, he was temple-worthy. But Billie learned that inside he was a broken boy, having been brought up in a toxic home, with a weak, abusive father and a schizophrenic step-mother, whom he hated.

"He would intentionally call me Shirley, his stepmother's name."

It didn't take long for the cruel and emotional abuse to start. But she became pregnant, and the babies arrived, three in four years. In addition, David joined the Coast Guard in order to receive veterans benefits, and they moved often.

Billie sought guidance from the Church. What she received was advice to "fix" herself.

One of the things that bothered David was Billie's weight gain.

"I had weighed 132 when we got married. Over the course of three pregnancies, I had gained at least fifty pounds. I became a size sixteen.

"If you would lose a few more pounds, you would not be so disgusting to me," he said.

David was emotionally abusive to the children as well.

"His thing always was you must be stoically strong, no matter what— any weakness was not tolerated. He would be aggressively, mercilessly mean."

On one occasion he decided we all should take karate, the Japanese martial arts. The kids were working for their first student belt. The belt was awarded to them by the instructor. When we got home, David was livid.

"I have no idea why you got that belt. Your form was bad. You didn't deserve them."

He threw all the belts away.

Another occasion of deliberate cruelty toward one of the children happened when Billie and David were away.

"My oldest son was a geek. He did a chemistry experiment in the living room and blew up the couch, hurting himself. He had crystals in his eyes, and a friend took him to the hospital. When we got back in town, we went to the hospital. My son looked like he had the crap beat out of him—his face and eyes were in terrible shape. My husband started yelling at him, telling him he was going to teach him not to do experiments. David said he was going to shave his (son's) head."

"He took delight in humiliating the children."

"It made no sense to me who I was then. I was the perfect definition of learned helplessness. I had flashbacks of who I was as a child in the mountains. How had I strayed so far from that child who loved life so much?"

She knew she had to find a way to leave the marriage and support her children—she would return to college. His response was predictable.

"If you get a job or go back to school, I will leave you. You can't survive without me."

"I had no knowledge or cultural permission to learn how to change my situation," Billie said.

Again, she talked to leaders in the Church, but all they could tell her was that she had to try to "right herself."

How could she right herself when it was obvious she was married to a very sick man?

The Extrication and Rebuilding

Billie re-enrolled in college and took computer programming classes.

"My whole life was just this messy, miserable thing. With FORTRAN programming, the basic computer programming course being taught then, you figure out how to solve problems: do this, then this, then this, and things are black and white. Here was a world in which everything is structured. This is what I needed."

"One day I came home from visiting my mother to find that David had accosted my middle son, thrown him against the wall and twisted his arm. He was hiding under a pile of clothes in the closet. The other son was hiding out in the bushes. My daughter had run away.

She said to David, "You crossed the line." She knew the end was near.

But first there would be one more move. With her father's encouragement, they moved from the isolation of a rural Oregon home with no running water and an outhouse in the forest to Las Cruces, New Mexico, where her father lived.

My father loaned us his yellow banana-mobile—an old Chevy Impala. She remembers the very last time being a passenger in the car with David, driving at about thirty-five mph.

"I don't remember the specifics, but he was screaming at me—I couldn't stand it any longer. I opened the passenger door and jumped out of the moving car. I was fortunate I wasn't hurt."

She told him he had to leave the home, and he went to stay at a hotel. She filed for divorce.

"He sent flowers."

It was too late.

"I only stayed with the Church because of my husband. When we divorced, he left the Church too. But the Church abandoned him because the leaders did not know how to support him, the primary emphasis being on supporting the sacred family relationship."

Mother and Daughter Struggles

The Mormon Church teaches that when you leave the Church, you leave God. Exaltation to godliness comes when the nuclear family stays together in the next life. By leaving the Mormon Church, "I was guaranteeing that I would not live with my mother in the next world."

But by the time of the divorce, Billie's mother understood the reasons for it.

"She was confused by my marriage, because David was the picture of the good Mormon man. But he had treated her badly too. He wouldn't allow her to hold the children when they were babies. 'This is my baby,' he said."

Over the years, Billie's mother had become more fragile.

"She was always needy. She grew up in an environment of poor white trash and carried that self-image. She always competed with me and wanted what she wanted when she wanted it. She wanted to be honored and be taken care of.

"In her upbringing, children moved two streets down, and there was constant interaction; but our nuclear family blew up, and the kids were everywhere.

"She had expectations of what a daughter should be like. As the matriarch, she felt she had to force people to give her what she wanted—I was the one who could be guilted into doing things for her."

"But there had always been dysfunction. Her desire to protect herself had been great. It never mattered what my needs were. She probably learned all of that from her harsh childhood."

In the end, Billie had to put physical distance between her and her mother. Her mother's emotional need for attention was suffocating her.

After leaving the Mormon Church, Billie did not want to leave her God. She was terrified. She still loved the Lord.

But she had one recurring thought: "I figured that the Heavenly Father didn't want me to be miserable for the rest of my life."

Then, one day she heard a voice: *I have been with you since the day you were born, and I will be with you until you die. Don't be afraid.*

She believes she has always had spiritual guidance.

"It's a very funny thing. The person who I am now is the same person who was running around in the backyard as a child. I think the closer to God you are in truth, the process of coming close to God means you are becoming the real person, and interacting with Him reveals the truest self.

"Freedom means looking at the world as you see it, taking in the information, and having to reintegrate the information in the most honest way. The interesting part is how you can do that and still be a Christian."

The New Checklist

By the time, she met John at work, Billie had her bachelor of science degree in computer engineering, with a minor in math. He was an engineer too. She had ballooned to a size eighteen. Her children were having all kinds of problems as a result of their abusive home environment, and Billie was trying to eat her way out of stress.

"My daughter got into some trouble with drugs, and the court had given her permission to live with her father. That didn't work out.

"There was a time when she would run off with people she didn't know. We didn't know what happened to her, but it turned out to be really bad stuff.

"She became an alcoholic and developed a fatty liver—she almost died.

"But now she has dumped alcohol and cigarettes and has control over her life."

Billie's new checklist for a man in her life had on it how a man treated people.

"How he treated the most powerless people in the work environment. And how merciful he was." Billie watched how John interacted with everyone at work.

"He pulled up everyone around him, and I knew he was exactly the person who was right for me. I would go days without eating because of stress related to the children. He would come in and get me burritos to make sure I was not going to take a dive.

"He had to dig through layers of stuff to find the real Billie."

In the end, they both found the person with a heart they were looking for.

Wheelchair Bound

Things got better with the children, but, there was still the question of weight. At one point, Billie, at 5'6" weighing 205 lbs. had a tremendous amount of back pain. She recalls having to crawl from one room to another at home, because the pain was unbearable when she was upright. She envisioned spending the rest of her life in a wheelchair.

In 2006, she quit work and had surgery for a disintegrating vertebrae.

"The surgeon was able to reconstruct the vertebrae so I was strong enough to walk, but there was scar tissue; every time they scraped it away, it would come back. It wasn't very long before I was struggling to move around again." She continued to be in pain that six separate occasions of physical therapy would not relieve.

"But the compounding problem was continuing use of pain medication—the opioids of fentenyl and hydrocodone."

She became addicted.

There was only one solution. She had to take the weight off to lessen the back pain. But first, she had to walk away from the narcotics.

The Tucson hotel room was nondescript, standard stock: a bed, a desk, and curtains that closed. It served its purpose. Billie didn't want anyone to see her go through withdrawal. The room gave her the anonymity she needed. She paid for a week, not knowing how long it would take. She laid on the bed for twenty-four hours, shaking, sweat soaking her clothes.

Round one. One opioid down.

Billie and John purchased a home in Sahuarita, Arizona, where the next episode of withdrawal from the second narcotic took place. Billie came to the house alone, leaving John at the farm with the animals.

"I closed all the blinds, laid on the floor, and got clean."

On both occasions, she prayed for God's help, at times wondering if He had abandoned her.

Round two. Opioids gone.

The Weight Loss Program

The location of the home Billie and John purchased in Sahuarita in a fifty-five-plus subdivision was a strategic decision—it was a block from the fitness center.

"When we started, we looked like Mr. and Mrs. Clause. We pledged to go twice a day to the center to use the exercise equipment.

"We kept our promise. It took a year, but the weight came off."

"But we had to change our diet too. We cut way back on sugar and our portions. We ate more vegetables."

Part of Billie and John's workout was using a step platform to do aerobics to music, something they had done on their lunch hour at the worksite years earlier. At first, they were the only two in the aerobics room. Then, another woman asked if she could join them. The woman suggested that Billie seek permission to teach a class there. The answer was yes.

Billie stands at the front of the aerobics room behind her step platform. She wears a two-inch silver cross on a chain around her neck and is comfortable in her lead role. Last year her hair was short and graying; this year, it is short and a deep rust color. In most social occasions, she says, she is profoundly introverted, never initiating a conversation with people she doesn't know.

This teaching adds value to Billie's life in three ways:

1. "I have come to know these women. You see others worse off and filled with courage. They are reaching out to grab life.

2. "Being kind to people is a core value I am able to fulfill with this class.

3. "It gives me a sense of purpose, and it almost feels like a calling—like serving a mission."

Today Billie's new life is full of self-reliance and grit, and her personality developed in a spirited childhood remains strong. Filled with gratitude, she is leading others into the light through healthy living, believing she is far removed from darkness and closer to God than she has ever been.

She's also pretty sure she knows why God forced her to go through withdrawal twice by herself instead of spontaneously healing her. She was recently treated for a knee problem and given a prescription for pain—a narcotic.

"I never got the prescription filled. I knew what I had gone through, and I said *never again.*"

THOUGHTS AND THEMES: REGIONALISM, RESILIENCE, AND ROOTS

Over the course of writing this book, friends and the women profiled here have asked questions about the identity of my women. When I was in Arizona interviewing Billie Qualtrough about her Mormon beginnings, she asked about the other women profiled. I told her about Carol Crocker Harton, born and raised in the inner city of Detroit. "Oh good. I don't know anything about inner-city life," she said. Alternatively, I knew my Michigan friends wouldn't have a clue about Billie's life either.

I asked my Michigan friends how many Mormons they knew. If they were close to my age, they remembered Governor George Romney from the 1970s; if they were younger, they knew of his son Mitt Romney. But for the political lives of the Romney family, they knew no Mormons and had no knowledge of the history of this Christian denomination. My Wisconsin friends were the same. They knew of only one Mormon: Mitt Romney.

I have come to realize how much geography can govern our knowledge base. People in the West probably know more about Mormons. People in the East may know more about the Underground Railroad.

For those who, like me, have spent most of their lives in cities and suburbs, women's lives on the farm may be eye-opening. While many baby boomers know about life in post-WWII America, knowledge of European life during and after World War II may be new to them.

At the conclusion of my writing, I was still curious about resilience. How is it these ordinary women, each so different in their own right, experienced some pretty extraordinary moments and moved on? For the answer I turned to the definition of resilience: Adapted well in the face of adversity, trauma, tragedy, threats, or significant sources of stress.

A review of studies indicates that exposure to intermittent stressors made individuals psychologically tougher, becoming less overwhelmed by subsequent difficulties. So stress-free upbringings are not necessarily a good thing. Those who have had some adversity are higher functioning and more satisfied with their lives than those who had experienced no adversity.

A friend of mine was not convinced this is a subject worth writing about. "But, Sharon, all people have overcome some kind of adversity. What's the big deal?" she exclaimed. Clearly, other people have had worse lives. But these eight are the women who showed up in my life, having overcome rocky starts, toxic marriages, concerns about emotionally abused and starving children, and ultimately the loss of a child.

Finally, I know of no others who have lives so steeped in history with such deep roots in place and soil as Alice or a twenty-eight-year intimacy with a different culture as Connie.

Certainly not I.

This book is my means of honoring these ordinary women.

RESOURCES

Jayne Jaffe Jordan Profile

Helminiak, Jon. *This Token of Freedom: A Remarkable Wartime Journey.* Bloomington, IN: IUniverse, Inc., 2012.

Summers, Julie. *When the Children Came Home: Stories of Wartime Evacuees.* London: Simon & Schuster UK, Ltd., 2012.

Ina Zeemering Profile

Sellin, Thorsten (ed.), "The Netherlands During German Occupation," *Annals of the American Academy of Political and Social Science,* Vol. 245 (May 1946) 1-180. https://222.jstor.org/stable/242853

Van der Zee, Henri A. 2016. The Hunger Winter. Google Books. https://books.google.com/books?hl=en&lr=&id=?_eNGEV_QL64C&oi=fnd

Zhao, Xiaojian. 2016. "Immigration to the United States after 1945." Oxford Research Encyclopedia of American History. Oxford University Press. doi:10.1093/acrefore/9780199329175.01.

Sheila Kersey Harris Profile

DeRamus, Betty. *Freedom by Any Means.* New York, NY: Simon and Schuster, 2009.

Froner, Eric. *Gateway to Freedom: The Hidden History of the Underground Railroad.* New York, NY: W.W. Norton & Company, Inc., 2015.

Frost, Karolyn S., and Tucker, Veta S. (eds.). *A Fluid Frontier: Slavery, Resistance, and the Underground Railroad in the Detroit River Borderland.* Detroit, MI: Wayne State University Press, 2016.

Hill, Lawrence. *The Book of Negroes: A Novel.* New York, NY: W.W. Norton & Company, Inc., 2007.

Tobin, Jacqueline L., and Jones, Bettie. *From Midnight to Dawn: The Last Tracks of the Underground Railroad.* New York, NY: Random House, 2008.

Alice Barlass Profile

Apps, Jerry. *Whispers and Shadows: A Naturalist's Memoir.* Madison, WI: University of Wisconsin Press, 2015.

Sanders, Scott R. *Staying Put: Making a Home in a Restless World.* Boston, MA: Beacon Press, 1994.

Rock County Historical Society Archives

Gladys "Rusty" Deland Profile

Markel, Howard. *The Kelloggs: The Battling Brothers of Battle Creek.* New York, NY: Pantheon Books, 2017.

Constance Fletcher Profile

Beck, David M. 2005. A Struggle for Self-Determination: A History of the Menominee Indians since 1854. https://books.google.com/books?hl=en&lr=&id=7TjT40nwkhwC&oi=fnd.

Menominee Tribal Enterprises, Our History: MTE History. http://www.mtewood.com (accessed 2/1/17).

Carol Crocker Harton Profile

Michigan State University Archives

Detroit Public Library, Burton Collection

Billie Pase Qualtrough Profile

Lyman, Edward L. "Elimination of the Mormon Issue from Arizona Politics," 1884-1894, *Journal of Arizona and the West* 24(3), 205-228, 1982.

Maraniss, David. *Once in a Great City: A Detroit Story.* New York, NY: Simon & Schuster, 2015, 224-228.

Sletten, Carol. *Three Strong Western Women.* Wolf Water Press: Pinetop, AZ, 2012.

Stott, Clifford L. *Search for Sanctuary: Brigham Young and the White Mountain Expedition* (Vol. 19), Salt Lake City, UT: University of Utah Press, 1984.

Wariner, Ruth. *Sound of Gravel.* New York, NY: Flatiron Books, MacMillan Imprint, 2017.

Welker, Holly. *Baring Witness: 36 Mormon Women Talk Candidly about Love, Sex, and Marriage.* Urbana, IL: University of Illinois Press, 2016.

Thoughts and Themes

Jay, Meg. "The Secrets of Resilience, What does it take to conquer life's adversities?" *Wall Street Journal*, November 11-12, 2017.

CPSIA information can be obtained
at www.ICGtesting.com
Printed in the USA
LVHW050083711021 9
607105LV00006B/433/P